HANS HOLZER

THE DIRECTORY OF
PSYCHICS

How to Find, Evaluate, and Communicate with Professional Psychics and Mediums

CB

CONTEMPORARY
BOOKS

A TRIBUNE NEW MEDIA COMPANY

Library of Congress Cataloging-in-Publication Data

Holzer, Hans, 1920–
    The directory of psychics : how to find, evaluate, and
communicate with professional psychics and mediums /
Hans Holzer.
       p.   cm.
    ISBN 0-8092-3561-7 (pbk.)
    1. Psychics.   I. Title.
BF1024.5.H65   1995
133.8—dc20   95-15911
                                                CIP

A portion of the material in this book was published previously in
Predictions: Fact or Fallacy? and *The Prophets Speak.*

All insert photos © 1995 by Hans Holzer
Cover photo by C. C. Cain Photography

Contents

Introduction

Currently there seems to be a renewed interest in things paranormal. During the late seventies and the eighties, when "times were really good," fewer people felt a need for psychic or spiritual guidance, perhaps because of the country's embrace of materialism. But whenever the economy takes a downward course or the world seems unstable and threatening, some people look to voices from beyond—in the hope that the gifted ones will tell them that soon things are bound to get better.

What makes the present quest different are the technological advances that not so long ago were simply part of science fiction. As people seem to accept that before long we will actually be able to explore far-off galaxies, discover how the mind works, and learn how life begins, it does not seem farfetched to think that some clever people will be able to bend the space-time continuum and reach out into the tomorrow that is not yet or cross into the territory beyond the horizon.

Although it is gratifying to live among an ever-increasing group of people who take seriously such issues as ESP, telekinesis, and life beyond this world, it's unfortunate that some of the queries that I receive about contacting other planes come from persons who should be kept away from mediums and psychics. These may be emotionally unstable persons to whom any contact with the psychic world would only be a crutch to help them avoid facing up to the reality of drab or unresolved lives. I am very cautious about recommending a reputable psychic to people who need a counselor instead of a psychic reading, and frankly I wish to protect my medium friends from them.

Other calls, equally undesirable, come from youngsters who are looking for a new thrill. I do not approve of experimenting with Ouija boards and making a party game of what is essentially a field of serious scientific inquiry.

Most of the people who want to consult a good medium, however, have a sincere interest in the psychic field or perhaps a fascination with the occult, which to them is much like any other form of study and inquiry, and they deserve a hand. I am always willing to open the psychic door to sincere people, whether or not they fully understand the nature of the psychic world.

None of the mediums with whom I have dealt or sat does his or her psychic work primarily for the money. (If you want a fortune-teller for your party, you should consult an entertainment bureau, not me.) It is entirely reasonable, however, to receive compensation for one's services, and psychic services are no exception. A minimum of $50 per hour would be a fair price. Some wealthy individuals give more; and poor ones, less. In Great Britain, where the regulation and collection of fees is handled by the London headquarters of the Spiritualist Association, mediums themselves have nothing to do with bookings or money. Members of the association are charged a flat fee for a sitting, regardless of the medium consulted or the time involved.

A *trance medium* has the ability of "total dissociation of personality." A trance medium can slip out of his or her own body and allow another person to inhabit it temporarily in order to come directly into contact with the spirit personality.

In a sitting, an intermediary is usually, but not always, present—acting as a guide or a control on the nonphysical side of life. This "master of ceremonies" introduces the discarnate personality that comes to speak and also closes the sitting at the end. Sometimes in the course of a reading, the control of the trance medium or the discarnate friends or relatives of the sitter will make predictions, but predictions are not the main purpose of trance mediumship.

The ability to work in a trance is a rare gift, and a trance is a very taxing ordeal for the medium. I know of no more than a half dozen genuine deep-trance mediums whom I would consider excellent. (A number of clairvoyant mediums claim or think that they are trance mediums, but they are merely deluding themselves.) Trance mediums usually do not make themselves available to the general public for private sittings, but there may be exceptions—as, for example, when a person comes as a researcher or when a person has been properly introduced by someone known to the medium. Trance mediums, who prefer to concentrate on research, are averse to being used, or abused, as fortune-tellers.

Undoubtedly there are trance mediums of whom I don't know; some may be in the formative stages, and others may simply not realize that they have this rare—very rare—gift. I can personally vouch for the ones I have listed here. Mediums who think that they may have the gift for trances but would like to make sure or who wish to develop their talent should get in touch with me. I am forever on the lookout for likely prospects. Trance mediums are needed, and really fine psychics in this most advanced phase of mediumship are too few. The majority of psychics, readers, interpreters and so forth are clairvoyants, or mental mediums, who perceive their impressions through their minds.

On occasion I have suggested one of the psychics listed in this book to people who have inquired about psychics for personal reasons if I felt that their interest was above the level of mere curiosity or that they had some truly important problem. Mediums should not be consulted as a lark because one is bored or because the thrill of it all will make marvelous conversation.

The pages of the tabloid press as well as popular magazines contain countless listings of people professing to be anything from gifted mediums to healers to occult practitioners.

Undoubtedly some are genuine and honest, but one wonders what to think of the fellow who, for example, advertises himself as "bishop" of his own church (a one-man institution, of course) or of a person who will solve all of your problems by mail at one dollar per problem.

It has always puzzled me how a magazine, like *Fate*, proclaiming an enlightened editorial policy of friendly skepticism can accept such drivel as advertising matter. But the quest for monetary gain has never stopped at the gates of the psychic world.

As the interest in consulting paranormal practitioners spreads, so does the attraction to the field of people who are not gifted in any way as readers but who see psychic practice as a quick way to enrich themselves in a profession in which controls are nonexistent. They practice at the price of defrauding their clients, but more important, they damage the reputation and public perception of psychics who are gifted and honest.

In this book, I hope to shed a bit of light on how we can all benefit from the remarkable powers of authentic psychics and mediums, for indeed there do exist people with extraordinary, *real* gifts for looking into other dimensions for answers to our questions. I also aim to offer some concrete advice on determining whether a "psychic" truly has psychical abilities and might therefore be of service to us. Unfortunately, in this day of 900 telephone numbers, "psychic networks," and other potential scams, a person who advertises himself or herself as a medium may simply be another con artist looking to prey upon our trust and hopes for personal profit.

I hope that you, my readers, will find this information of value in your personal quest for guidance, enlightenment, and wisdom.

Professor Hans Holzer, Ph.D.
New York, March 1994

What Exactly Is a Psychic?

A psychic (medium, reader, clairvoyant) is a person who practices the art of divination on the basis of his or her gift of extrasensory perception (ESP). ESP can be described as an innate energy force, which may be possessed in varying degrees.

ESP is neither miraculous nor supernatural; it is only puzzling to those who believe in a universe that can be fully apprehended by the senses of sight, hearing, touch, taste, and smell. Such a limitation does not allow for the possibility that psychic phenomena can take place; when they do occur, they must be explained in a fashion that is consistent with that limited view of the universe. Of course this method of rationalization is not realistic. The entire range of observed or experimentally induced psychic phenomena defies the traditional view of our world and cannot be squeezed into the narrow parameter of our ordinary five senses.

In order to understand what a psychic is and does, one first needs to understand what ESP is.

ESP may be defined as the ability of some individuals to obtain information that is beyond the limitations of the space-time continuum. In simple terms, the ability to perceive something that couldn't possibly be perceived under known laws of cause and effect must be attributed to a different phenomenon, a different power from those powers associated with the five senses. Originally, it was thought that humans had a sixth sense that made it possible on certain occasions for selected individuals to pierce the space and time barriers and come up with extraordinary results.

The idea of a clearly differentiated sixth sense was advanced by Professor Joseph Rhine, the pioneer in parapsychology whose early experiments at Duke University set the mood and tone for the years of experimentation that followed. Rhine investigated the mysterious sixth sense in humans by studying two factors: ESP, meaning the ability to circumvent or contradict the space and time laws, and psi, pertaining to psychokinesis, or the ability to influence solid objects by the power of the mind. Rhine's original experiments were carried out in association with Dr. Hornell Hart. Later similar experiments were conducted by Professor Robert McConnell of the Department of Physics at the University of Pittsburgh. Today, Rhine-type experiments are conducted at many universities, the original tests having become almost classical examples of ESP research. In order to test ESP, Rhine devised a special deck of cards illustrated with symbols such as squares, circles, and triangles. People who undergo the test attempt to guess ahead of time the sequence of the cards; over the years, many subjects have been able to do so. Despite elaborate studies and impressive statistics, however, the results have remained inconclusive. Subjects have foretold the exact run of cards in a specific deck; but some very psychic individuals have been total failures in the laboratory while less-gifted ones have done extremely well. On the other hand, the same people who failed the card tests have sometimes set impressive records in the open field with "spontaneous phenomena." Continued testing with cards can be boring; consequently, attention diminishes and performance diminishes. Without the subject's emotional involvement, it appears that predictable results cannot be obtained over any great length of time.

In addition to the card tests, The Rhine laboratory developed psi machinery with which to research the potential influence of mind over matter. In these experiments, the fall of dice is used to determine the psychic ability of the operator: the subject is told to wish for a given number to turn up on one or more dice, and the dice are then rolled by machine. The machine, a cage of transparent material containing obstacles that cause the dice to jump around, is turned by a motor and stops by itself. "The only human contact is the hand that flicks the switch to start the motor," explains Monroe Fry in an article entitled "Unsolved Mysteries of Psychic Phenomena." After years of testing with thousands of subjects, the experimenters concluded that in order to have paranormal manifestations, (1) the subject had to have a desire or a need, (2) ordinary channels of communication had to be absent, and (3) the subject had to be free of any psychological block.

Through the years a great number of spontaneous cases of ESP and psi were brought to the attention of the Duke laboratory, but very little of this material was followed up by on-site investigation. This lack of followup was partly due to lack of funds but also to a determination on the part of the original investigators to stick to laboratory methods and to try to present orthodox scientists with the desired repeatability of psychic phenomena. In a futile attempt to repeat phenomena at will in the laboratory, much valuable impetus was lost; in the end, it was clear that the impact of spontaneous psychic phenomena was much greater than the impact of these produced in laboratory experiments. It also became increasingly clear that the traditional rules set up to study physical phenomena would not apply to the observation of ESP and psi phenomena. New rules as well as new tools had to be devised in order to comprehend the vast amount of psychic data that would be presented to science.

Unlike standard scientific tests of physical phenomena, in psychic experiences human emotions are always involved: the phenomena do not occur unless someone is deeply involved, consciously or unconsciously, in their production; and the absence of emotional impetus has a marked influence upon the test results. In addition, under no circumstances can such conditions be produced in the laboratory except by hypnosis. Even by means of hypnosis, however, genuine ESP phenomena were not produced in the laboratory in sufficient quantities or at a sufficiently high level to convince scientists who were already skeptical of the entire field. The more scientists clamored for instruments to measure ESP, the more elusive the phenomenon became. Clearly, only the apparatus of the human personality was adequate to serve as a vehicle for the mysterious power. A minority of scientific observers then switched from futile laboratory experiments to the observation of natural phenomena when the frequence of occurrence made it feasible.

While American scientists were still debating whether ESP was a real force in humans, and if it was whether it could be reproduced in laboratory experiments, Russian scientists were way ahead of the game. Assuming that ESP existed, they wanted to know how to harness it, how to deal with it, and how to make it work. Not at all concerned with the method they would use to reach their goal, they started at the top, so to speak, by using actual sensitives in loosely controlled experiments that were a far cry from those conducted in the austere surroundings and the clinical atmosphere of the American laboratory. As a result, the Russians have come up with startling revelations, including photographs of actual psychokinesis in which objects are shown to be moved a considerable distance by the power of the mind; and they have initiated even more sophisticated experiments, going beyond ESP into the realm of psychic photography.

The very fine elements that make up the channels of telepathy are in fact physical but of a different density than the gross physical body of man. In my view, ESP is not a separate sense but rather the ability to go beyond what we currently consider the *limits* of our five senses. What we attribute today to a sixth, or extra, sense may well be considered part of our ordinary five senses. If anything, humans may have *five* extra senses— an extra range of the senses of sight, hearing, taste, touch, and smell. Activated by certain emotional conditions, we are able to extend the perceptions of these senses beyond their known boundaries. This ability is not a freak of nature, an exception granted by some superior power to a select few or developed only through strenuous and protracted methods. It is the birthright of every one of us, which can be dealt with in one of three ways: it can be ignored, it can be suppressed, or it can be enhanced.

If we ignore them, incidents of ESP in our lives will not go away but continue to intrude at various intervals. Ignoring them merely begs the issue: we will remain puzzled, perhaps even frightened, by them, and the result will be unsatisfactory from the point of view of both knowledge and mental outlook.

By suppressing incidents of ESP, we may create false personality traits. Whether we are motivated by social, religious, or scientific pressures, suppressing genuine incidents of ESP is not conducive to a balanced state of being, nor will suppression result in the phenomena ceasing altogether. By resisting what we consider an undesirable invasion of psychic forces, we may temporarily succeed in closing ourselves off from psychic vibrations or influences, but we cannot do so permanently. Spontaneous phenomena are bound to occur in our lives from time to time. We cannot possibly prevent them from happening; all we can do is to refuse to evaluate them, force ourselves to look the other way, give ourselves alternative, safely acceptable explanations. In a manner of speaking, suppressing ESP incidents is nothing less than fostering a falsehood upon ourselves.

Finally, enhancing our power of ESP is likely to increase not only the frequency of our ESP experiences but also the impact of individual occurrences. The first step toward the encouragement of receiving psychic phenomena is to accept these experiences as natural. Our outlook, then, must be directed toward the acceptance of ESP as a natural human ability and the absence of ESP as an affliction of sorts. By opening ourselves up to possible incidents, we are actively encouraging their occurrence. We are not manufacturing them, and we are not drawing them upon us; ESP phenomena cannot be invoked by merely wishing them to occur. Even in experiments, an emotional need has to be present for telepathy to take place between two subjects. In the case of experiments, the experimenters' somewhat more limited desire to succeed is at times sufficient to cause telepathy to occur, but such incidents cannot compare in intensity with the very real power behind spontaneous telepathy in an emergency situation.

To define once again the term ESP, we should remember that it is the ability to partake of psychic phenomena of all kinds: anyone who has had even one psychic experience, has ESP. Anyone who obtains specific information about events or individuals with whom he or she is not familiar in the conscious state has ESP. Anyone who obtains glimpses into the so-called past or future without consciously being able to do so shows evidence of ESP.

Knowledge that cannot be reasonably or adequately explained by perception through one or more of the five senses must be attributed to extrasensory perception. Of course, this knowledge must be specific, reasonably detailed and of a kind that could not have been obtained through telepathy from another individual present.

There seems to be no marked difference between the ability to pierce the dimension of time and the ability to pierce the dimension of space. In a way, both dimensions are alike. Likewise, there seems to be no difference between ESP into the future and ESP into the past. In fact, the dimension of time may not exist at all, and what we are dealing with may be an accommodation to make the dimension commonly called time more acceptable to our way of reckoning. This appears to be borne out by the fact that events seem to be stationary in this timelike dimension and it is we who move toward events.

In psychic research phenomena are divided into mental phenomena and physical phenomena. In mental phenomena, which include clairvoyance, clairaudience, clairsentience, telepathy, and psychometry, ESP is the driving force. In physical phenomena, principally trances and materializations, psychokinesis is the driving force, but ESP may be present.

Clairvoyance is the power or faculty of discerning objects not present to the senses, that is, of "seeing" beyond the boundaries of time and space. A clairvoyant may see into the future or into the past and may observe simultaneous occurrences in either. Some clairvoyant phenomena involve distance in both time and space; others, in only one dimension.

Clairaudience is the power or faculty of hearing sounds not present to the ear but regarded as having objective reality. Auditory phenomena may be from the present, the past, or the future; they may originate in the immediate vicinity of the clairaudient or at a great distance. Clairaudience is much less frequent than is clairvoyance.

Less frequent still is the ESP phenomenon called *clairsentience,* one form of which is the registration of specific scents for which there appears to be no logical reason. Because they represent associations both with people and with places, these scents communicate certain meaning to the recipient. They may be from the past, the present, or the future; like other forms of ESP, they may be from a geographic distance. Clairsentience usually occurs as a secondary manifestation along with clairaudience or clairvoyance.

Psychometry is the function or power of divining facts concerning an object or its owner through contact with or proximity to the object. Psychometry is based on the theory that emotional events create a thin film that permanently coats all persons or objects in the immediate vicinity. A psychometrist coming in contact with the persons or objects will be able to read the coating and thus will be able to reconstruct the emotional event. Most psychometry concerns the past, some of it bears on the present, and occasionally it will pertain to the future. Some psychometrists need to touch an object that has been on the person to be investigated, while others get stimuli simply by being in the immediate vicinity of the person. Professional mediums have been able to locate lost persons by touching objects belonging to the persons and reconstructing their immediate pasts. In some as yet little understood fashion, inducing agents such as personal possessions may also be used to make projections into the owner's future, thus making psychometry useful in crime prevention and other branches of detective work.

Telepathy, or mind-to-mind communication, is probably the best-known form of ESP. Telepathy works primarily between living people, but communications allegedly have taken place with the dead as well. Telepathic thoughts or images are transferred from one mind to the other. The message is encoded, sent through space at great speed, received by the mind of the recipient, decoded, and brought to consciousness. The entire process is almost simultaneous, but some time does elapse, since tiny amounts of electromagnetic energy are transmitted through space from one person to another.

More than any branch of ESP, telepathy may be achieved by inducement, that is, of willful attempts to make it work. In many ways telepathy resembles the process of radio transmission. Frequently the experimenter's strong desire to succeed is a sufficient impetus to create telepathic communication. Depending upon the relationship between sender and receiver, the communication may be partial or complete. The closer the emotional ties between the two individuals, the more likely it is that the results will be satisfactory. "Being in tune" is not a mere figure of speech but a very real condition enhancing telepathic communication.

Often clairvoyance, clairaudience, and telepathy overlap.

Clairvoyance, however, can never be induced—it is always spontaneous—while telepathy can be induced or planned.

A person is either asleep or awake. In the sleep state, which constitutes roughly one-third of the time spent on the physical plane, the threshold between the conscious and the unconscious is very low, making it easier for telepathic material to enter the receiver's unconscious mind. Consequently, much ESP material is received during the sleep state. The advantage is that with the obstacle presented by the conscious mind removed, more of the message can be absorbed. The disadvantage is that the receiver may forget part of the message or that symbolic or psychological dream material may intrude upon the ESP material, become mixed up with it, or in some way alter its purity. We have little control over the way we receive ESP material from others. Thus far, it has proved to be impossible to send material while asleep.

Despite some extraordinary happenings that indicate a close relationship between thoughts and action, ESP does not cause people to act in certain patterns or cause things to occur. A person who receives certain thoughts or impulses through ESP may react to them, but ESP does not give one person power over another in the way that hypnosis does. Esp is both a power and channel of communication. It has many facets, appears in many forms, and works best on the unconscious level. Operating somewhat like an electromagnetic current, it depends upon a sufficient supply of energy in both the sender and, to a lesser degree, the recipient. Like all psychic forces, however, ESP powers do not diminish with use but rather, in some not fully understood way, increase with use. The more we use ESP, the more we have. Above all, ESP is not a miraculous power that is given to a chosen few; it is not something that can be bought or acquired in mind-study courses alone; it is an innate human force, frequently left dormant because it is not understood. Its development should be taught in schools along with the three R's; and perhaps in the not-too-distant future, it will be. Whatever else it may be, ESP most certainly is not *super*natural.

Perhaps the most tantalizing aspect of ESP is its application to the foretelling of future events. It stands to reason that nothing interests one more than to know what lies ahead, whether for oneself or for one's community, whether for a loved one or for the larger world, for that knowledge may make it possible to prepare oneself.

Knowledge of events that are taking place in the present, even if at a distance, are less dramatic. True, Swedenborg told his audience of the great fire in Stockholm while hundreds of miles away the fire was actually raging. The effect was most dramatic, but his audience realized that they could do nothing about such a fire and that it would take some time before the truth of the statements could be confirmed.

The ability to delve into the past and describe conditions with which one is not normally familiar may be technically related to the ability to foretell the future, but knowledge of the past does not hold the same interest as does the quest for tomorrow.

Past events and past experiences cannot be altered. We may be able to change our attitudes toward them, but that involves only personal changes. We may be able to make some adjustments to events in progress (storms, wars, and so forth), but in general the only area where we can take action based upon ESP foreknowledge is in future events.

Another aspect of ESP makes the ability to foretell future events more controversial and tantalizing than any other: the ordinary person cannot perceive an event that has not taken place—and often cannot even conceive of it; yet hundreds of thousands of people have described in great detail situations and happenings that came to pass only at a later date. If this is true—and research has amply borne it out—then our concept of time and the sequence of events are subject to revision. Quite clearly, if a significant number of people can foresee and foretell future events far beyond the law of chance and far beyond guesswork or generalities, then either our sense of time is wrong or the events themselves are predestined by some superior law with which we are not yet fully familiar. It is very difficult to judge such matters from within our accepted framework of time and space. One must therefore construct a theory that would explain ESP experiences pertaining to the future, and at the same time satisfy our basic concepts relating to a three-dimensional physical world.

I will examine the nature of time later on, but for purposes of the discussion of foretelling future events, let it be stated that time is a human convenience, adopted in order to have a reference point; to a large degree events are predestined by a system that I prefer to call universal law.

Precognition is clairvoyance relating an event or a state not yet experienced. The majority of precognitive experiences occur spontaneously. Some people may have an inkling of a precognitive experience shortly before it occurs by feeling odd, having a sensation of giddiness, having a tingling in various parts of the body, or simply having a vague foreboding. To others, the experience is surprising and unexpected.

Many clairvoyants find that the ability to foretell events is more a burden than a blessing because they begin to believe that their foretelling of bad events may in some way be connected with their causing them. This, of course, is not true. By tuning into the existing conditions and picking up that which lies ahead through ESP, the receiver is merely acting as a channel and has no responsibility for the event itself, its outcome, its timing, its result, or its moral implications. The receiver has no more control over that which he or she foretells than a radio has control over the programming coming through it. I have a number of letters from people who think that they are "evil witches" because they have foreseen in exact detail an accident or the death of a friend or a loved one. They wonder whether their thoughts caused the event to occur, especially in cases in which the relationship between the psychic and the victim was unpleasant. There are cases on record in which thought concentrations influenced people at a distance, even made them do certain things that were not of their conscious will, but these incidents required a deliberate effort, usually that of several people working together, and lacked the spontaneity of the ESP flashes that are generally associated with true precognitive experiences.

Actually, the ability to look into the future is a progressive ability that we all have. It starts as a primitive instinct, as when one senses danger or love or warmth and reacts accordingly; develops into intuition, in which one's inner voice warns of danger or somehow vaguely makes one react with caution when faced with dangerous individuals or situations; and at the higher stage where actual ESP begins becomes a hunch. A hunch is a basically illogical feeling about a person or a situation that may influence one's thinking and actions. Following a hunch means to go against purely logical reasoning. If the hunch turns out to be correct, one has had a mild ESP experience. If it does not, it may not have been a hunch at all but fear. The two are very much alike. Fear of failure or fear of a confrontation may frequently masquerade as a hunch. The only way to tell the two apart is by the sense of immediacy, the sudden appearance and the short duration of the true hunch. Fear is a lingering feeling.

Beyond the simple hunch there lies the ability to foresee or foretell actual events or situations, called precognition. Whether the foreknowledge concerns events that occur a minute later or a year later is of no importance. The dynamics involved are the same, since one is dealing with a dimension in which time as we define it does not exist.

There are different stages or degrees of precognition. First of all is the situation in which one foresees or foretells an encounter with either a situation or a person without "getting" any specifics about time and place, mainly receiving only the basic message. When it occurs in the dream or sleep state, this simple precognitive experience may be surrounded by, or couched in, symbolic language. For instance, in a precognitive dream, your brother has bought a new car, which he wants to show you. The following day he phones to tell you that he is going to visit you in the near future. When he arrives, it turns out that he has just remarried and wants you to meet his bride. In the dream the car was a symbol for the new wife. When the receiver is in the waking condition, however, descriptive material is much more precise; even though not every precognitive experience contains the desired details of time, place, and description, the absence of material from the unconscious mind allows the message to be much clearer and more precise.

Next comes the precognitive impression in which a time or a place element is present; the indication may be only partial, such as a numeral "flashed" above the face of the person in the vision, or a key word spoken by an inner voice that relates to the circumstances of the future event. Depending upon the personality and the state of relaxation of the receiver, the precognitive message will be partial or more complete. If it is merely routine, although it may be of some emotional significance to the receiver, the message is less likely to contain dramatic descriptive material than if it concerned a catastrophe, a dire event, or a situation of importance to more than one person. For instance, clairvoyants who are able to predict plane crashes (a specialty among some) do so in great detail. The same appears to be true for those who predict fires and earthquakes. The curious thing, of course, is that not all such occurrences take place as predicted. This, however, is not due to the inaccuracy of the vision or precognitive experience but, because it comes from a timeless dimension, to the visionary's misjudgment of the time element.

There remains the question of whether the person with ESP foresees the future in the presence of a specific individual or not. If a number of seers independently make precognitive predictions about a particular individual in their presence, then the future event must cling to the aura or electromagnetic field of that individual. If, on the other hand, the seers are not in the subject's presence when they foretell such events, then it would seem that the person has opened a channel into future events in which he or she merely plays a part but over which he or she has no control.

Anyone who doubts the existence of precognition need only consult the records of psychical research societies throughout the world for detailed descriptions of cases that have been carefully recorded over the years.

A premonition is a milder form of precognitive experience in that it is usually a feeling about an event to come rather than a sharply defined flash of an actual scene. Premonitions are much more numerous than the more complex form of precognitive experience. In a 1969 article, entitled "Can Some People See into the Future?" published in *Family Weekly*, Theodore Irwin reported that a London piano teacher named Lorna Middleton had a strong premonition concerning the fate of Senator Robert Kennedy. Nine months before the assassination Ms. Middleton felt a strong premonition that Kennedy would be murdered. On March 15, 1968, she saw the assassination take place and felt it was while the senator was on tour in the West. This impression was followed on April 5 and April 11 with forebodings of death connected with the Kennedy family. The actual murder took place on June 5.

As a result of frequent press reports about premonitions, a psychiatrist named R. D. Barker set up the Central Premonitions Registry, where people could register their premonitory feelings. The greatest impetus toward some sort of registration of premonitions came after a huge coal tip buried the Welsh village of Aberfan in October 1966, killing 138 people. Many people in Great Britain had reported premonitions of the disaster, some even giving the exact time and manner of occurrence. Among those who had an inkling of the catastrophe was my good friend Michael Bentine, the writer and comedian, who had scheduled a TV sketch dealing with a Welsh village on the fatal day. For reasons that he could not explain, he canceled the sketch at the last minute.

Barker thought of the registry not only as an instrument to prove scientifically that people do foretell the future but as a kind of clearinghouse to warn of impending catastrophes. To be this, of course, it was necessary to prove that a significant percentage of the premonitions were actually coming true. During the year 1967 469 separate premonitions were filed. Of those only eighteen proved to be accurate. Twelve of them were made by two individuals—the aforementioned Ms. Middleton and Allen P. Hencher, a forty-five-year-old telephone worker.

"They are absolutely genuine," Barker was quoted in *Family Weekly*. "Quite honestly they stagger me. Somehow these sensitive people can gate-crash the time barrier—see the wheels of disaster starting to turn before the rest of us. It is difficult to attribute their experiences to coincidence alone."

Taking a lead from Barker, several Americans also attempted to set up premonition registries. Among them were Dr. Stanley Krippner, clinical psychologist and director of the Dream Laboratory at Maimonides Medical Center, Brooklyn, and a young sensitive named Richard Nelson. Unfortunately, the majority of people who have premonitory experiences never bother to register them with anyone because most concern disaster or negative aspects of life. Receivers are afraid to bring bad news and frequently prefer to dismiss their impressions or actively suppress them. As a result, much valuable psychic material is undoubtedly lost to science, and where there might have been warnings, and possibly prevention of disaster, there are only the faits accompli.

The British sensitive Allen Hencher has been quoted as follows regarding his premonitory experiences: "Most of the premonitions come while I am working, maybe because there is a lot of electricity at the telephone switchboard, yet they also come at night, when the air is clear, or after a glass of wine. Usually my premonitions are accompanied by headaches, like a steel band around my forehead, but as I write them down, the headaches recede. When I feel that a premonition has been borne out, I feel utter relief. It is as if something had been bottled up in me."

Probably the most surprising hunch recorded by Hencher, one quoted widely in the British press at the time, related to an airplane accident. Hencher had been awake all night because of an ominous headache and during that time clearly foresaw an airplane crash in which there would be 124 victims. In his telephone report to Barker the next morning, Hencher described the scene as reminding him of Greece and gave details about some statuary around a church. Instinctively, he felt that the place was Cyprus. Several weeks later an airplane crash on Cyprus killed 124 people.

"Our notion of the dividing line between present and future is probably incorrect," Krippner said. "We interpret the present as being the exact moment when something is going on. In reality, however, the present for an event may come within a wider span of time. There are forces at work now that will probably not become obvious for a year or two. Then, when an event does take place, in retrospect we realize that it is part of the present."

Helen Ann Elsner of Iowa worked as a nurse's aide in various hospitals and as a laboratory assistant in animal research. Her paranormal experiences usually take the form of a premonitory dream. As a child Elsner had a recurrent dream in which she saw a specific drugstore and a dime store in an unfamiliar town. When she was staying in Grand Falls, Canada, in the summer of 1958, she suddenly recalled those dreams. She felt compelled to walk into the town and to her surprise found the very two stores that she had so often seen in her dreams. From that moment on, the dream has not recurred.

As a child Elsner also dreamed about a three-story mansion with a long curved stairway leading into the main living room. Years later when she was a missionary student in Lowell, Massachusetts, the house she went to live in was exactly like the house that she had seen in her childhood dreams. In the summer of 1961, Elsner was a medic in the Women's Army Corps stationed at Fort Belvoir, Virginia. In the cafeteria of the military hospital, she met a corpsman named Jackson. About two months later she had a vivid dream about him that stayed in her mind. In the dream Jackson was in patient's pajamas and she was the hospital aide taking care of him. She was straightening the covers of his bed as part of the evening care when he reached up and tried to kiss her. At that moment a woman walked into the room and Jackson remarked, "There's my ex-wife. I did not know she knew where I was, let alone sick, because we are divorced." On that note the dream ended. Several weeks later when she saw Jackson in hospital pajamas in the cafeteria, Elsner immediately recalled her dream. Jackson asked her to come to his ward. As she was standing by his bed talking about a book she had read, he looked up and inter-rupted. "There is my ex-wife," he said. "I didn't know she knew where I was, let alone sick, because we are divorced." How could Elsner have guessed or in any way foretold Jackson's exact words on that occasion, especially since she lacked the funda-mental knowledge concerning Jackson?

Only by tapping the future can we explain incidents of this kind, which are indeed numerous. Sometimes a sensitive sees events that are near in both space and time. In November of 1972, Elsner was driving home from work at about six o'clock. As she neared Twenty-fourth Street in the town of Ames, Iowa, she could not get it out of her mind that there would be an accident scene ahead. She took this as a warning and drove very cautiously for the next few blocks. When she got to Twenty-fourth Street, she found the scene that she had pictured in her mind: two wrecked cars, three police cars, and an ambulance.

Elsner has learned to live with her gift. Her ESP not only

warns her of disaster but helps her in minor ways as well. The trouble is that she has very little control over it. "Sometimes when I am shopping," she explains, "I get that certain feeling or urge to go to a certain store for whatever it is I want. Sometimes I have to look for a long time in that store, but I have always found the article. The sad part is that this feeling is not voluntary, it comes only when it wishes, and if I push the issue I may go wrong."

Some professional mediums have almost made a career out of predicting catastrophes. Shawn Robbins, a woman whom I personally trained as a medium, has an impressive accuracy record in the prediction of airplane crashes.

John Gaudry, a young man who has worked with me on several occasions, gave me a written statement on January 20, 1971, concerning a dream he had had the night before: "I saw a rather large helicopter crash into cold waters, either a bay or river. It was painted either orange or red and was a cabin-type helicopter. People were splashing around in the water but seemed to be able to make it. I fear this may happen within the next few days and within the New York area." Four days later, the New York *Daily News* reported that a helicopter piloted by Apollo 14 backup pilot Eugene Cernan had crashed with terrific impact into a river and burst into flames while the astronaut was making simulated lunar landings. Cernan was picked up by a passing boat and rushed to a nearby marina. Later he was examined by physician John Teegen and was pronounced unhurt. Although he was wrong about the area in which the accident would occur, Gaudry had described the scene pretty accurately.

Is there any training that we can use to enhance our ability to foretell the future? First of all, people who have had some indication of this talent are more likely to be able to do something about developing it than those who have not. In either case, the technique to be used is much the same. Basically, it consists of remaining in a watchful state when one has any indication, no matter how slight, that they are going to have a premonition. Nothing must be ignored; everything should be written down. If possible, as soon as it is received, reputable witnesses should be alerted about the nature of the premonition. Also, if possible, one should write a letter concerning the experience and send it to oneself by registered mail, thus permitting the postmark to serve as a guarantee concerning the time of the prediction. As to increasing one's ability to have premonitory experiences, the attitude should be one of acceptance about any potential material, pleasant or unpleasant. Absence of fear and a certain objectivity concerning the material are equally necessary. Morally one is required to pass on whatever information is received, whether it is good or bad.

If specific information concerning the future is wanted, there are certain inducing agents that may work. If one is seeking information about another person, perhaps a photograph or the person's name written clearly on a piece of paper may serve as a concentration point. Having visualized the person or thing about which one wants information, one settles back into as relaxed a state as possible and concentrates upon the mental image. In this respect, the process resembles meditation except that a precise channeling is taking place. Tangent thoughts should be dismissed, and the mind should not be allowed to wander. Another approach might be to go to the place—a house or some other location—about which one seeks to obtain precognitive material.

By and large, precognitive experiences come to one unsought and unexpected. In sharpening one's general ESP abilities and streamlining one's concepts about ESP, one indirectly increases the frequency of spontaneous premonitions.

When a major precognitive experience concerns a large segment of the population or even an entire country, we speak of prophecy. The advantage of such material is that it is of interest to a much larger group of people than are personal predictions or premonitions. The disadvantage is that it involves public figures and problems about which almost everyone has some conscious knowledge. Thus the annual ritual, so dear to the heart of journalists, of predicting events in the year ahead is nothing more than a farce. Since the mediums consulted are selected at random, usually in brief telephone interviews, the predictions given are indeed vague and general. It is not too difficult to make some fitting prediction about a big movie star or the president.

Whatever predictions concerning public figures are made, physic researchers should insist on specific details regarding dates, places, and circumstances. If possible, the prediction should contain information that is not generally known. Perhaps the classic example of a prediction involving a public figure is the record of Michael Nostradamus, the sixteenth-century French physician and seer, who enjoyed the confidence of the French kings. Nostradamus's predictions were couched in poetic language and written in quatrains as a matter of safety at a time when witches were still being put to death and any-one possessed of ESP was considered a witch. In the 1560s Nostradamus went on record as predicting that a future king of France named Henry IV would be assassinated on a certain highway by a schoolteacher, whose name he also gave. Some fifty years later, the assassination took place as described. When Nostradamus made his prediction, neither the king nor the murderer had yet been born.

Nostradamus spoke of airplanes, submarines, and atomic warfare as if he knew about them intimately. His predictions included one of a terrible great war after which there would be a "government of England from America." At the time the term *America* did not exist. Nostradamus also identified Adolf Hitler by name and gave a correct description of what was to transpire during his lifetime. Students of prophecy should take as yet unfulfilled predictions of the French seer very seriously.

The answer, then, to the question of whether we can fore-tell the future must be in the affirmative; at the same time, we should realize that we cannot turn this ability on at will, nor can we regulate it even partially. At best, we can observe ESP competently and draw certain conclusions from it, not so much about ourselves but about the nature of the future and our role in the scheme of things.

Just as the future is not yet when viewed from the present, the past is no more. Artifacts from distant periods in the past may remain, but the past itself is gone. The people in it and the events shaping it no longer exist in the physical sense of the word. There is, however, one basic difference between the past and the future: the future is not yet, when seen from the present, and therefore cannot be apprehended by the five senses. Having existed, the past, on the other hand, has left a record. The difficulty in coming to terms with the expressions *future* and *past* lies not so much in the limitations of our five senses as in the terminology we are forcing ourselves to use. By assuming the existence of three distinct segments of time—past, present, and future—we arbitrarily cut a steady flow of consciousness into distinct and artificial units. In actuality, the progression from past to present to future is continuous and uninterrupted. In essence, past, present, and future are of the same stuff. The divisions between them are artificial and flexible. The only proof that something has become objective reality—that is to say, has already happened—comes from observation of the event. Even if there were no witnesses, the event would transpire just the same. Thus when we speak of the past, we speak subjectively: it is the past as seen from our individual points of view. Our observations may be similar, but they are nevertheless individual observations and reflect the past only because the observers are at a later juncture in time than the observed event. Perhaps it would be more correct to speak of such events as accomplished events rather than past events.

By contrast, future events could be characterized as unrealized events. From the point of view of the observer, past events have occurred and can no longer be altered; future events, which exist independently, have not yet occurred in relationship to the observer and in some instances may conceivably be altered.

In psychometry, we derive impressions about events that have taken place prior to our experiments from persons, objects, or places. These impressions are always emotionally tinged; purely logical material does not seem to survive. The emotional energy that accompanies traumatic events "coats" people, objects, or locations and contains the memory banks of the events themselves. In touching a person or an object that was in the immediate vicinity of an event, we are merely replaying the event in the way that a phonograph replays a prerecorded record. The events themselves do not possess any active life, and the reproduction is quite faithful, subject only to the limitations of the transmission and the personality of the receiver. Therefore, the message may contain part or all of the original event; it may come through correctly or partially correctly; or it may be a mixture of event and personal interpretation, since, after all, the receiver is a human and not a machine. But the process itself is basically impersonal and should work equally well for all events and in all experimental locations.

In psychometry, then, we see and interpret a kind of emotional photograph of past events. In reconstructing the event through the psychometric impulses and with the help of our conscious mind, we are not actually re-creating the event itself but merely developing an imprint or copy of it. This, however, is sufficient to derive information about an event and thus learn facts that may otherwise be lost in history. Some years ago, in a book entitled *Window to the Past,* I showed how a medium could be taken to historical "hot" spots, places where puzzles in history had not been fully solved, and attempt to solve them by means of psychometry. Sybil Leek was thus able to pinpoint the actual locations of Camelot in England and the first Viking landings on Cape Cod, Massachusetts.

Psychometry is a valid and very valuable tool of historical exploration and can undoubtedly be used much more than it has been in the past when other means of historical research fail. To be sure, the information obtained through psychometry is not to be used verbatim to fill in gaps in history but is used as a departure point for conventional research.

A second method of visiting the past is through astral projection, also called an out-of-body experience, in which our inner self, the etheric body, temporarily leaves its physical abode and travels, usually at great speeds, into space. Although astral projection is ordinarily into space and not time, it is quite possible to direct an astral projection into a predetermined segment of past history. It works better if done at the location that one aims to investigate, but it can also be done from a distance. The success will depend upon the person's power of visualization and the absence of interference from conscious or unconscious sources. Induced astral projection should not be undertaken alone but only in the presence of a competent observer, who can suggest that the person travel into a particular region of space and time and that he or she should recall all of the information obtained there upon return and awakening. Astral projection is accomplished by lying on a comfortable surface, preferably at a time of day when the body is reasonably tired and relaxed, and by gently suggesting an outward motion of the inner etheric body. Closing one's eyes while suggesting to oneself the lowering of the threshold between conscious and unconscious minds initiates an outward floating, which will eventually become a physical sensation. The inner self may leave the physical body through the upper solar plexus, at the crown of the head, or through the stomach area. Return of the inner self to the physical body is accompanied by a sensation of rapid deceleration—experienced as a kind of free fall—of spinning, and occasionally by an unpleasant feeling of having fallen from a great height. This sensation, however, is due only to the rapid speed at which the etheric body reenters the physical body. The process takes place in a comparatively short time and can therefore be momentarily unpleasant, but is in no way dangerous to either mind or body.

Somewhere on the borderline between astral projection and psychometry lies what the late Eileen Garrett called "traveling clairvoyance." In traveling clairvoyance a part of the medium is projected outward and is able to observe conditions as they existed in the past without the inner self actually leaving the physical body. This talent is found primarily in professional mediums. It is not easily acquired.

Hypnotic regression as used in reincarnation experiments also propels the individual into the past. Such experiments, which should always be undertaken under the supervision of a professional hypnotist trained in parapsychology, may result in the obtaining of information from past incarnations that can be verified independently afterward. With regression, it is always better for the hypnotist to suggest to the subject that he or she will not retain the past memory upon awakening so as to avoid any traumatic residue. Thus, the only information about the past that is available to the researcher is the information that is brought by the subject while he or she is in a hypnotized state. Since with hypnotic regression the concern is more with personal experiences in past lives than with historical exploration, the thrust of the investigation is somewhat different from that required for purely past-oriented research.

A number of instances are on record in which people have accidentally entered a "time warp," that is, an area in which a different time stream was still extant. In one such case, a young man who was driving from northern Oregon to California suddenly found himself at the bend of a road in a blizzard, although he had left in August when the weather was extremely hot. For what seemed to be a full day, he found himself in a mining town among people dressed in the clothes of the early 1900s. He vividly remembers speaking to the people and finding them to be three-dimensional. Suddenly he was seized with panic and, regaining the safety of his automobile, drove away, to the bewilderment of the entities he left behind. Shortly afterward, he found himself back in the present and the relative comforts of a hot August day.

One must not classify such experiences as hallucinations, even though hallucinations are possible with certain individuals. In cases of this kind, the material obtained during the incident is the crux of the explanation. In the case of the young man, the detailed descriptions of his encounter seem to indicate that he had indeed entered a time warp of sorts. Whether the experience was due to his own mediumistic abilities or to the location at which it occurred is difficult to assess. But from time to time similar cases have been reported, in which people, and even vehicles, from the past have been observed amid contemporary scenes only to vanish a few moments later or to return on other occasions or to other observers. Scenes from the past are not unlike ghosts except that ghosts are tied to specific locations and personal fates and these scenes seem to exist independently and include a variety of individuals. We do not know why some of these scenes from the past have "hung around" while the majority have faded away. All of the cases known to me have had emotional connotations; thus I feel that unresolved emotional problems may have kept such scenes in existence. Perhaps someday we will devise an apparatus to replay historical occurrences at will.

Albert Einstein pointed out that energy cannot dissipate but must continue to exist even if it is transmuted. Is it not possible that the emotionally tinged scenes—which, after all, represent energy—exist in a dimension not ordinarily accessible to us for observation? On occasion, however, certain individuals are able to penetrate this dimension in which past events continue to move on a different time tract from the one we have created for our own convenience.

Walking into the past, then, is both a matter of choice and

a matter of accident. Either way, the past is far from dead and continues to intermingle with our present. Probably the most common form of "reading" the past history of a person or a place is done through the kind of ESP that permits a medium to tell facts about a person or a place without having access to any information about, or any previous conscious knowledge of, the person or the place. Since the ability to read the past is a very common talent, we must assume that the past continues to exist all around us; that is, the past exudes tiny particles of itself, and persons who are sufficiently sensitive to it may derive information from its emanations.

Many scientifically minded individuals will readily accept the reality of ESP and at the same time strenuously reject the possibility that the human personality survives after physical death. Whereas ESP may be viewed as an extraordinary faculty possessed by some individuals, the idea of an existence beyond death involves a religious concept and may be discounted in the face of considerable evidence.

Many of the phenomena attributed to ESP in its various forms—from telepathy to psychometry, even clairvoyance and the ability to look into the future—can be explained without the need to assume a world beyond this one. Most of these ESP phenomena involve living people, and although they may fall outside the accepted laws of cause and effect, these incidents nevertheless do not imply the existence of another order of things that would necessitate a radical rethinking of one's philosophy. But when we come to the question of ESP communication with the realm of the dead, we are opening a Pandora's box. If there is such a thing as communication with the so-called dead, then our biological concept of life needs to be greatly modified. Nearly all "establishment" scientists, especially in medicine, postulate that the physical body of humans is nearly all there is, with the mind being a personality complex rather than an invisible but actual unit. Until the establishment of psychiatry and later psychoanalysis as recognized sciences, the concept of a mind separate from the body was as unacceptable to such scientists as the concept of another dimension beyond death is to them today.

Perhaps the strongest reason for difficulty in accepting the existence of a world of the dead is the seeming invisibility of that realm. Trained to accept only the evidence of our five senses, we find it difficult to give credence to a set of conditions that cannot be measured with those senses. We are forced to go by assumptions, deduced from the testimony of others, and to work with material that is acquired indirectly rather than by the direct approach, so useful in dealing with physical matters, of working with concrete evidence. But this is merely prejudice on our part. Many areas of human knowledge are based upon invisible values: we know that an electric current can accomplish certain things, and we can measure the results; but we cannot actually see an electric current flowing through a wire. Even if we touch the wire and receive a shock, we are merely experiencing an effect of the agent and not the agent itself. When electricity is conducted through certain substances, such as gases, we can photograph the path of an electric current, but we cannot photograph the current itself.

Magnetic waves cannot be seen by the naked eye nor can they be touched; but they can be measured by sensitive instruments, and their effects can be verified. Perhaps an even better parallel lies in the causative agents of disease. Microbes were not known until the invention of microscopes sensitive enough to reveal them. Illness was attributed to a variety of factors ranging from the will of the gods to human accident.

We will be able to understand the workings of the etheric body in humans a great deal better once we have perfected instruments sensitive enough to measure that body. At the present time we can only assume that an etheric body exists because we see it at work in psychic phenomena. It seems, as the late Bishop James Pike might have put it, "the best of several possible alternatives." We have photographed the human aura, the electromagnetic field that extends beyond the human skin and indicates, among other things, the person's state of health. We have measured and studied the tiny electrical currents going through the nerve fibers of the brain, and we know that the electroencephalogram does not lie; electricity does go through the nerves. We can look at the heavens and see only a tiny portion of the bodies in space simply because our instruments are not refined enough to see them all. This does not mean that additional worlds do not exist, but only that we have not yet been able to reach out that far. It is the same with "inner space": our inability to record objectively the very fine elements making up the etheric body should in no way be confused with the absence of such a body. Everything in the study of paranormal phenomena indicates that an etheric body exists in humans. Taken as a whole, the phenomena generally associated with ESP cannot be explained better than by assuming that a person possesses an inner power that is capable of breaking through the time-space barrier and accomplishing seemingly paranormal phenomena. The phenomena are in fact perfectly normal; they appear extraordinary only because of our lack of comprehension. In Procrustean fashion, we make the observed facts fit the established theory instead of building a theory upon existing facts. This cannot, of course, go on forever; the scientific establishment is bound to revise its criteria of evaluation when the pressure to do so becomes unbearable.

The haphazard and surprising way in which communications from the dead are received by the living, the suddenness of apparitions, the voice in an empty room that is identified with a deceased person who was known to one, visits from long-dead relatives and friends, farewell messages at the time of passing—all of these phenomena, which are very common indeed, might not be so numerous if we the living were not continuously bombarded with a philosophy of living based upon false values and false information. Only a small minority are prepared to consider communications from the dead natural and desirable. Perhaps the need of the dead to manifest themselves to the living would be less compelling if we lived in a world in which the existence of channels between the physical world and the next dimension were no longer in doubt.

As I have pointed out through many examples published before, the purpose of the majority of the communications from the dead is to acquaint the living with the continued existence of the dead in another dimension. Whether the dead person wants to make amends for his or her own lack of understanding of this dimension in his or her own lifetime in the physical world or whether the dead person wants to educate a living one who is ignorant of this dimension for the latter's own benefit, the fact is that many "dead" persons have a compelling desire to let those whom they have left behind know about their world, in which they continue to live a useful and seemingly complete life.

Scientists who are unfamiliar with the material on this subject tend to shrug off apparitions of, or voices from, the dead as hallucinations. Putting the blame on the observer, they suggest that either the phenomenon did not take place at all or it was due to the observer's emotional and psychological malfunctioning. This explanation may hold true in a small number of cases and may be a possibility in some other cases in which an element of mourning exists, but it certainly does not hold true in cases in which a deceased person has made a "surprise visit" to an individual who did not know that he or she had passed on or who did not know him or her at all and later had to ascertain the identity of the apparition from independent sources. Such cases, in fact, make up the majority of the apparitions observed by sane, sound individuals and told to reliable witnesses or registered in the records of reputable research societies. People stay at houses and are surprised by the apparitions of dead individuals about whom they know nothing. Later, on checking their experiences, they find that they have seen dead persons who were formerly associated with the particular houses. People are visited by strangers who claim they are long-dead relatives; on checking with family members, the identities are later established. People report the appearances of dear ones at the very time that the people are dying or have just died, without, of course, any knowledge of the time or the place of death. Such experiences are well established and documented in the files of such research societies as the American Society for Psychical Research, the British College of Psychic Sciences, and for that matter, my own very extensive files. That there is another dimension close to this one in which we live I do not doubt in the least. This dimension seems essentially to be a thought world, in which specific electromagnetic fields contain the memories and emotional stimuli of individuals who were formerly alive. For all practical purposes, then, the dead are nothing more than the inner selves of living people, looking like them, thinking like them, feeling like them, and being able to move rapidly, since they no longer have to carry the weight of a physical outer layer called the body.

The people who have had experiences of this kind with the dead run the gamut of professions, ages, and national and educational backgrounds.

Sally G., a registered nurse in Georgia, reported the following experience:

> In the past I worked with the National Institute of Health in Bethesda, Maryland. I mention this because it was there in the Institute of Neurology that I was taught to note and describe full details. . . . At the time of this incident I was living in the same town with my mother, but my two children and I lived in a house that was several blocks away from my mother's house. My husband, Captain M. G., was at that time serving another tour in Vietnam. My brother, Captain Joseph D., was in Army Intelligence in Vietnam when on

February 28, 1967, his plane crashed and burned. The pilot and my brother died instantly.

Several months after my brother's death, my mother fell and broke her hip and dislocated her shoulder. Naturally she had to be hospitalized, and when she returned home about a month later, she had to have around-the-clock help. When this incident I am about to relate occurred, she was not in the house alone but had a practical-duty night nurse who was then in the living room. My mother's apartment was on the downstairs floor. At the time she had her bedroom door closed and her room was definitely darkened as she had always been a light sleeper and was sensitive to noise and light. She was lying in bed and was beginning to feel very relaxed, although she was not yet asleep, when the room suddenly seemed to be illuminated and sort of "pressurized." Then she saw her son, Joseph, standing near the foot of her bed, smiling at her. She could see him as clearly as if it were daylight.

There followed a brief conversation between mother and son, in the course of which Mrs. D. asked Joseph how his father was and he replied that his father, who had passed away four years before, was fine. The vision then disappeared, but Mrs. D. could still sense her son in the room with her. She began to tremble and to cry. She called out to her night nurse. Since the door was closed, the nurse couldn't hear her, so Mrs. D. picked up a small object from her night table and threw it against the door. The nurse, Mrs. F. S., came into the room, where Mrs. D. was now crying uncontrollably. When the nurse entered the room, Mrs. D. cried out, "Oh, Mrs. S., Joseph was here." To her surprise, the nurse replied, "Yes, I know. I saw a brown shadow go past the dining-room table."

The following morning Mrs. D. became somewhat calmer after informing her daughter of the event of the night. Shortly after she had had her nursing care, Mrs. D. went back to bed with the intention of taking a nap, since she had been awake so much of the previous night. As soon as she was alone in her room with the door shut, her dead son reappeared suddenly and said to her, "Mother, I am sorry that I frightened you last night." Then he disappeared again. This time, however, Mrs. D. was not upset. For one thing, it convinced her that she had not dreamed the incident of the night before. There was no doubt about it; the apparition had been that of her late son, Joseph. He had appeared quite solid, not transparent, as legendary ghosts usually are. Mrs. D., under questioning by her daughter, stated that Joseph had been dressed in civilian clothing, a shirt and pants. Mrs. G. thought that that was significant because although her brother was an army career man, he had been bitter toward the service at the end and would have wanted to appear in civilian clothing on his last journey.

William Hull, of Brooklyn, New York, is a member of an amateur theatrical group called the Promenade Players. Here is his statement, dated August 17, 1970:

> During our last show, our director, Joan Bray, became quite ill, and, in fact, nearly died. Joan loves to entertain, especially us in the group, but because of her illness had not been able to most of the summer. On July 31 of this year she felt good enough to have us over for dinner. She invited half of the group on Friday and the rest for Monday, August 3. Because he had moved and not left a phone number, she had not been able to contact Chuck Taylor, our lead in the last show. While she was preparing dinner on Friday afternoon, the thirty-first, Chuck called and in a characteristic manner asked when he would be invited over for dinner. Joan told him he could come either that evening or the following Monday. He replied that he would much rather come when he could eat alone with

Joan and her teen-age daughter. Joan didn't think this request out of the ordinary as Chuck was a person who was always "on stage" with a group but liked to relax and was a different person when he was alone with someone. So no definite date was set, but Chuck did give Joan a phone number to reach him at so that she could invite him when she felt like it. Then, in closing the telephone conversation, Chuck made an unusual request: "Take care of yourself, Joan," he said in a rather sober voice. Joan replied that of course she would. "No, I really mean it. Take care of yourself," he repeated. Again Joan replied that she always took care of herself. To placate him, Joan promised and this ended the conversation. Joan didn't think about the conversation except to mention to those of us that asked that she had heard from Chuck and he had left a number to reach him.

About the twelfth of August a photographer friend of mine, also a member of our group, tried to contact Chuck to tell him that some long-ago ordered prints were finally ready. He discovered that Chuck had collapsed and died on the seventeenth of July. Of course, we thought that there must be some mistake, but by careful check we found that he had indeed died and had been buried on the twentieth. Now the only other explanation was that it was not Chuck that called that afternoon, but Joan Bray knew Chuck better than anyone else. Her long and close relationship with him seemed to rule out any possibility of an imposter calling.

Romer Troxell, the father of twenty-four-year-old Charles Troxell, whose body was found punctured with bullets and stripped of identification by a roadside in Portage, Pennsylvania, in 1970, can attest to the reality of communication from the dead. According to a United Press account, as published by the *Los Angeles Times* on May 30, 1970, the father kept hearing his son's voice directing him to the accused killer. It all started when he looked at the face of his dead son in the Portage morgue. "My son just simply spoke to me," the father is quoted as saying. "He said, 'Hi, pop. I knew you would come. He's got my car.'"

Since the police were tight-lipped about the investigation, Troxell and his family went to stay with Troxell's brother in Gary. Troxell became restless and found himself in his car with his wife and sister-in-law as if he were searching for something. His dead son, Charles, was guiding him. He was driving along a road that he had not been on before when he suddenly heard his dead son's voice say, "Here he comes, Pop." But there was just a hill ahead and no sign of any car. Then he saw the yellow Corvette coming over the crest, and Charlie told him, "Here he comes, Pop. Take it easy. He is armed. Don't get excited. He's going to park soon." The father followed the car, and as soon as it was parked outside a high school, he went up to the young driver, later identified as the murderer. "The boy knew who I was," the father continued. "He said he had seen my car at my brother's home." The boy claimed that Charles had sold him the car, adding that he had not seen Charles for two days. When the father asked, "Are you sure?" the boy said, "No, but isn't he dead?" Then Troxell knew he had the killer before him, since his son's identity had not been published in the newspapers, and it was known only to the police and the family. As the father continued his conversation with the young man, he again heard his son's voice saying, "Be careful, Pop. He's got a gun." Under the circumstances, Troxell decided to play it safe. He knew that the police, summoned by his sister-in-law, were en route. As soon as the boy had been arrested and charged with the murder, the son's spirit voice faded and has not been heard since.

Fully documented examples like these can be found by the

thousands. In communications between the living and the dead, whether initiated by the dead or by the living, the initiator uses the faculty of ESP to make himself or herself felt. Only if the recipient has sufficient ESP to convert the very fine emanations sent out from the nonphysical world can the conscious mind register the information. An emergency, an emotional necessity, or any kind of urgency will make the impact of the emanations much stronger. In the cases just discussed, the need to communicate was present. Ordinary communication was impossible. The majority of the communications from the dimension beyond the physical are initiated by the dead themselves; the recipient can only hope to be a good channel. The way to become a good channel is to put body, mind, and spirit into a relaxed state. When the body is relaxed, the nervous system is likely to exclude external interference and disturbances. By clearing itself of thoughts and becoming as blank as possible, the mind permits itself to become a receiver. By accepting the reality of such communications and the higher guidance that it implies, the spiritual self ties it all up in a neat package of possible breakthroughs.

To initiate communication with the dead by means of ESP is another matter. If there is a compelling reason for such communication, putting oneself in a state of receptiveness is, of course, the first step. If a specific contact is desired, visualizing the person on the "other side" of life may help. The dead cannot be summoned, however. You cannot reach out to them at will and command them to appear or to get in touch with you. At the very best, you can hope to set up conditions that would be favorable to their wanting to communicate with you. If your need is genuine and if you are in a relaxed, receptive state, then the communication may very well occur. Patience and a certain disregard of time are also valuable, since conditions that may appear favorable to us may not be favorable from the point of view of the person on the other side.

At any rate, the only means of communicating with the nonphysical world is ESP. Only thought forms can break through the barrier separating the physical and the spirit worlds. The stronger your ESP, and the more disciplined your use of it, the more likely it is that you will be able to have contact with those in the nonphysical world.

Physical phenomena are those that require some bodily action on the part of the medium or the sensitive. The manifestations are also observable in the conventional way and seem to rely upon energies drawn from living bodies, usually the body of the principal sitter or medium and the bodies of others in the immediate vicinity. Physical phenomena include deep-trance mediumship, teleportation (the movement of objects by mental powers), and materialization. In Professor Rhine's view, there are two main components of psychic phenomena: ESP and psi (psychokinesis). Rhine attributes the physical phenomena to the presence of the "psi force," by means of which a person can move objects by his or her mental efforts. In my own view, both ESP and the psi force are aspects of one and the same force: in an ESP phenomenon, mental results are obtained by mental effort, whereas in a psi phenomenon physical results are obtained by mental effort. If, however, we consider Einstein's theory that mass and energy are merely different aspects of the same force, then the difference between mental and physical phenomena narrows down even more.

In the case of deep-trance mediumship, the personality of the sensitive is temporarily displaced—voluntarily in most cases, involuntarily on occasion—by the personality of another, usually a deceased person. There are also cases on record in which an incarnate inhabited the physical body of a sensitive for the purpose of making a communication known, but the largest percentage of genuine cases of deep-trance mediumship involves communication between a discarnate, or dead person, and a living being, the medium. The medium serves merely as a channel of communication, allowing the discarnate entity to take over the speech mechanism of his or her body without being involved in the communication in any way. In a genuine deep trance, the medium has no memory whatsoever on returning to full consciousness of what transpired during the trance or of what words came through his or her mouth. In partial trances, which are common, some memory remains.

Although full materialization depends primarily upon physical factors, such as ectoplasm drawn from the physical medium and the sitters to cover the mental projection, materialization is in essence an ESP phenomenon. A discarnate's materialized body is maintained only by the discarnate's continuing ESP projection of his or her former self as he or she remembers it. The power that makes materialization possible is the same power that makes the projection of the living personality possible. In fact, there is never any basic distinction to be made between psychic phenomena in the living person and in discarnate states; the underlying principles are exactly alike. The incarnate personality within the physical body is identical with the latent etheric, or spiritual, body that is released to independence after physical death. In addition, some ESP is involved in materialization séances, since it is through their extrasensory powers that the sitters and the medium sense the presence of discarnates in the room. ESP is a factor primarily in the initial stages; once full visible materialization has been accomplished, the ESP phase is no longer necessary and generally ceases. In a marginal way, ESP has been quite useful to the researchers with a degree of sensitivity who went to a number of American spiritualist camps to investigate so-called materialization phenomena. In nearly all of the cases that they investigated, the researchers found fraud. Their inner feelings led them to suspect some of the principals in the sittings. In these instances ESP was not used to communicate, or make contact, with discarnates but was used purely as an extension of the ordinary senses to gain additional knowledge.

Teleportation, the act or process of moving an object or a person without contact by psychokinesis, has fascinated phys-

ical researchers for many years. Among common teleportation
phenomena is apport, the unexpected appearance or disappearance of solid objects. There is no doubt in my mind that
genuine apports exist and that psi power, the physical force
within humans, makes them possible. Whether the force is
directed by an external entity or the unconscious of a person
remains a debatable issue. In a number of verified cases, discarnates manipulated the apports. ESP is involved in teleportation only indirectly. The actual movement of the object is
due to psi, but a recipient on the usual ESP "beam" is aware of
and understands the meaning of the process.

In so-called direct-voice phenomena, a human voice is
heard. The voice is an objective reality that can, among other
things, be recorded on tape. Although the voice does not
emanate from the medium but appears to come "from thin
air," the manifestation of these phenomena does require the
presence of a strong physical medium. Although they are
related to the mental phenomena associated with ESP, direct-
voice phenomena are classified as physical phenomena, since
they are said to be made possible by a voice box constructed
from invisible ectoplasm. In the spiritualist séance rooms, especially of the 1920s, trumpets were used, allegedly to increase
the volume of such spirit voices. Frequently, the trumpets
floated in the air without visible support, and voices indeed
originated from them. Although a number of such séances
have been unmasked as fraudulent, an equally impressive number have been genuine: trumpets have indeed floated without
means of trickery or wires.

The psychical energies that are capable of maintaining a
metal trumpet in the air for a long period of time and of producing loud human voices that are obviously independent of
the speech mechanism of an entranced medium are not properly ESP energies, in the sense that Rhine would use the term.
Psi and psychokinesis are physical phenomena, utilizing other
aspects of the human personality and body than the mind.

Nevertheless, I doubt that psi forces could operate independently of ESP.

Teleportation usually takes the form of inexplicable disappearances and reappearances of objects and sometimes total
disappearances. In the majority of cases on record, the phenomenon seems to have no rhyme or reason, except, perhaps,
to attract attention. If we attribute teleportation to a split-off
part of a personality, of the subject himself, then we might
explain teleportation as an unconscious way of demanding
attention or working out submerged frustrations.

In Germany, an unexplained noisy or physical phenomenon is referred to as a *poltergeist* (ghost). In my view, however,
poltergeist phenomena are only the physical aspects of regular hauntings, or attempts at communication by spirits, and are
not caused by living persons alone. Conventionally, but incor-
rectly, such phenomena have been connected exclusively with
prepubescent young people; but they involve older persons as
well. A common denominator among persons who experience
poltergeist phenomena seems to be an unexpressed sexuality
that leaves the body a residue of unused life force.

Some of the witnesses to poltergeist phenomena are beyond
suspicion, keen observers whose testimony is of much value.

Mrs. M. Ball is a practical nurse with special training in
psychiatric work. She makes her home in the Middle West but
has also spent much time in California. She is now close to
sixty years old. From childhood, on Ball has experienced a full
range of ESP phenomena. Here is part of her report to me:

> Teleportation has been a nuisance to me all my life.
> Recently something of this nature happened to me
> which almost flattened me in surprise. On awakening
> from an afternoon nap, I found a greeting card on my
> chest. It was small in size, with tulips and lilacs on the
> left side. It was printed in a foreign language and con-
> tained a verse from Matthew 5:3 (the language was

Swedish). My house is always locked with double locks. No one could possibly have entered. The card could have entered the house in a book or newspaper, but it could not have located itself on my chest without help.

When I was in St. Louis in 1956, the keys to my bedroom and to the outside apartment door vanished almost while I was looking at them. I searched but found it impossible to locate them. I therefore could not get back into the apartment hotel in which I was staying and had to rent a room in a nearby rooming house. Three blocks away from my apartment hotel, in the rooming house, I placed my purse open on the bedside table and emptied it of all its contents. There was little in it to begin with. It was an inexpensive plastic purse without lining, with a drawstring closing. While it was sitting open on my bedside table, I had the sudden desire to check it once more. Just as I reached out to touch it, the keys fell with a clink, obviously out of the air. I did not see them fall, but I certainly heard them.

Four pages of a manuscript I had prepared at one time in the hope of selling an article to a romance-type magazine disappeared from the envelope on my dresser in Riverside, California. This was in a new, uncluttered room with no possibility of anyone entering. I had been home all day on a Sunday, and late that afternoon I went to make a final inspection of the manuscript in preparation for mailing it early the next day. I found the first four pages missing. They had been in place late Saturday evening. I looked through everything in that room, but the four pages simply were not found to be anywhere. Two hours later I was standing at a metal-topped card table, which was bare. Suddenly the pages, with an extra page from some carbon copies I had not seen for weeks, were lying on the table before my eyes. I had not seen them transported through the air, nor did I see any movement of any kind. They just materialized, face down, on the clean card table. One moment it was empty, the next the five pages of typed script were there miraculously.

The power that moved the keys and the manuscript was of course psi; but the intuitive process that made Ball look in certain places or be near a spot where the missing object would shortly be found was an ESP process, utilizing mental channels.

Teleportation phenomena cannot be induced at will, although a state of expectancy can be produced if a person is inclined toward physical phenomena. For the experiment, it would be wise to choose a quiet, not too bright room and to empty one's conscious mind of all extraneous thoughts. Once a state of repose is reached, one might project simple and direct requests for some proof that would tend to reinforce one's own faith in physical phenomena. A request for a demonstration from one's unseen friends is sometimes answered and sometimes not. It helps to be well rested, in excellent physical health, and not troubled by any problem or extensive worry.

To be sure, not every mysterious disappearance of an object is due to psychic causes. People do forget or misplace things or allow themselves to be victimized by others without realizing it. But there are a sufficient number of cases, similar to the ones reported by Ball, to warrant the statement that physical objects can be made to disappear spontaneously and reappear equally spontaneously in different locations. The pattern emerging from these phenomena seems to indicate that they serve a dual purpose: to prove that such phenomena are possible to begin with and to call a person's attention to the presence of some discarnate entity who wishes to be noticed and possibly desires to interact with the person.

2

How to Deal with Psychics

The first step in learning about the various forms of psychic activities is to consult directories such as this one or to listen to word of mouth, which in this field is particularly significant. But finding the appropriate medium is only half the job. If the reader is to derive full benefit from such an association, he or she should know how to behave, what to do, what not to do, and how to evaluate the result of the consultation. Perhaps the greatest problem in this field is the uncritical attitude of the individuals consulting professional psychics, coupled with a false expectation on the part of many, which makes it difficult to speak of universally acceptable results.

The medium or other psychic practitioner is only an intermediary between the person seeking a deceased personality or some information and that personality or information. The first thing to forget is the notion that the medium is some sort of supernatural being, possessing paranormal powers that make him or her capable of changing the world, performing seeming miracles, or otherwise behaving in contradiction to natural law. In earlier centuries, mediumship was frequently considered a special gift of God that was bestowed on very few, giving those who exercised it an aura of the supernatural. Sometimes psychics were almost worshiped; at other times the very same psychics were accused of being in league with the devil. In the days of the Old Testament, prophets were considered extraordinary human beings, somewhere between man

and God, certainly not ordinary citizens. Christianity has
tended to make mediumship either a saintly device (with the
mediumistic personality speaking as a vehicle of God) or a dia-
bolical instrument (with messages coming from the mediumistic personality being considered evil). Christianity hasn't
been able to place mediumistic individuals into a category of
their own, to accept psychic phenomena as natural forms of
human consciousness. Nearly every other religion has ascribed
special attributes to people capable of functioning as psychics,
ranging all the way from inspiration to divinity. Sometimes the
medium is referred to simply as a master; at other times the
medium is thought to be possessed by the deity itself; but the
notion that a medium can simply be a person with a particularly high degree of sensitivity to vibrations carrying thought
energies has not found acceptance in any religious establishment. It is only in the light of today's scientific understanding
that mediums are properly classed as individuals with sensi-
tivities greater than the average. We know that the dividing
line between sensory perception and extrasensory perception
is thin and flexible indeed and that being mediumistic is by
no means unnatural or supernatural.

It is well to remember that mediums are only persons with
a heightened sensitivity and thus not to approach a sitting or
a public reading with a sense of awe but rather with a healthy
curiosity and a balanced approach that allows neither for
extreme skepticism nor for uncritical belief. Always remember
that the medium giving the psychic reading is a professional
performing a service as well as he or she can, that the medium
may fail at times and succeed at others, that he or she may be
good with one person and not good with another, and that you
are dealing with a fellow human being not greatly different
from yourself.

Everybody is born with the gift of ESP. In some persons it
develops to a larger degree than in others; in some cases it is
encouraged through tolerance and interest; in other cases it is

ignored or suppressed. But the fact remains that ESP is not a mysterious sixth sense, as some would have it, but merely an extension of the five senses beyond the limits that we have erroneously been brought up to believe they have. ESP, or psychic ability, is therefore a natural function of all our senses. It is the absence of this faculty that makes us "subnormal," not the presence of it that makes us "supernatural."

In primitive societies, people have retained a large degree of psychic ability, and to this day those in some remote areas use telepathy to communicate with each other, in the way we use the telephone. Partly through a materialistically oriented industrial society and partly through social and religious prejudices, sophisticated modern man has to a large extent lost the natural ability of ESP. This is not to say that people cannot regain it by enlarging their environments to take in many aspects that were deliberately ignored in the past. Those who despite restrictive conditions maintain a considerable degree of psychic ability discover somewhere along the line that they have unusual gifts. Some of them turn these gifts into a profession. This is no different from, say, a musically inclined person's discovering his or her talent for the piano. Playing the piano can either remain a hobby for the amusement of one's family or, if perfected, become a professional way of life, a way to earn a living as a concert pianist or popular piano player. The choice is potentially everyone's, depending only upon environmental pressures, personality factors, individual likes and dislikes, or the potential acceptance by the public of one's professional activities.

If you have chosen a particular practitioner to consult, make sure that you do not give more than your name, and not necessarily your real name. I have often tested mediums by giving a fictitious name, only to find that the really good ones will get my actual name in the course of the sitting. I recall the late Lillian Bailey of London, of whom I had heard a great deal. In order to make sure that the test would be adequate, I refrained from communicating with her directly but asked the editor of the *Psychic News*, Maurice Barbanell, to make the arrangements for me. Barbanell called Bailey in my presence, asking her to arrange for a sitting with a certain Mr. Wood, for whom he could vouch. The personal assurance was necessary, since mediums are sometimes harassed by newspaper reporters who are disguising themselves as believers, or even by an occasional policeman who is trying to stir up trouble.

After I had arrived in her suburban home and taken a seat opposite her, Bailey went into a deep trance, and her control, a Scottish doctor, took over her speech mechanism. Within a matter of three or four minutes, this control exclaimed: "Why, you are not Mr. Wood at all. Your name is Hans Holzer." Needless to say, I was surprised. A hostile reporter would assume that the editor of the *Psychic News* had informed Bailey of my true name, but such was not the case, since Barbanell was as scrupulous in his work as he was reliable in his integrity.

Nothing would be lost if you were to give a false name, if that is your desire. However, if your name would have little meaning to a stranger, there is no need to do so. In my case, disclosure of my real name would have automatically disqualified any material received concerning my published career. In the case of the average individual, the medium is not likely to have any conscious knowledge of the person. If no address is given when one is making the appointment, even the remote possibility of a dishonest medium's checking up on a prospective sitter will be eliminated. In all the years I have tested mediums, I have never met a medium who went to the trouble of checking up on a sitter's personal circumstances. It is true that Spiritualists maintain cards concerning regular visitors to their camps and these cards are frequently passed from one medium to another in a fraudulent manner. But the material on these cards is obtained in routine sittings, and no one goes out of his or her way to collect a file on individual sitters for the sole purpose of defrauding them.

Very few psychics can do a full reading without sitting opposite the client, especially the first time. On occasion, I have
been given bits of information of a psychic nature on the telephone by such renowned mediums as the late Betty Ritter and
Ethel Johnson Meyers, but that, I think, was due to the fact
that we had sat together many times and a permanent link had
thus already been established between us. On first acquaintance, a personal visit is always recommended. People who
would like to take the easy route of obtaining psychic readings
by mail (or telephone) are only deceiving themselves. Psychics
who dispense such readings without prior personal contact are
either extraordinarily gifted or unusually cynical.

Once an appointment has been made, it should be kept—
and kept on time. Reputable psychics apportion their time very
carefully because they can do just so many readings a day.
Otherwise, they might endanger their health, and if not that,
at least their accuracy. Psychic work requires physical energy,
and that energy must be replenished through rest and sleep
in order to be readily available at full strength. Some mediums
can do as many as ten to fifteen readings a day, half an hour
each, only to fall exhausted at the end of the day. Others take
but a single client a day. It is difficult to set norms for such
work, since every medium knows his or her own strength.
Probably the safest number of readings per day lies somewhere
between two and six. Whether you are going to the residence
of the psychic reader or you expect the reader to come to
yours, the etiquette is the same. One should be as relaxed as
possible, ask permission if a tape recorder is to be used, and
not smoke unless encouraged to do so by the medium.
Incredibly, some mediums do smoke, and rather heavily,
although smoking is not conducive to their work. But then,
one of the best and most evidential psychic healers preceded
his work with extreme sexual activities, which he believed supplied him with the necessary "fuel" to perform his work.

It is a common and unfortunate mistake for a client to book

a psychic for consultation and then to go into the reasons for the consultation. It is understandable, especially if the reasons are compelling ones or are emotionally motivated, but by going into reasons, the client removes a large element of believability from the resulting material. The ideal appointment is made by giving only one's name, without any information about the nature of the business, the reason for the sitting, or anything else concerning the sitter.

It is not only all right but useful for you to exchange a few generalities with the psychic reader, especially if it is the first time that you have met him or her. This conversation relaxes both parties and sets up a vibrational bridge between you and the reader. The voice serves as a link, regardless of what is being said. Naturally, the conversation should not contain leading material that would be brought up during the actual sitting. You should never tell the reader why you are seeing her or him.

The initial conversation, which should not last beyond three or four minutes, could concern itself with the weather or with the difficulties or the lack of difficulty in reaching the place for the sitting; or it could touch on psychic research in general, books one has read, and so on. Personal business should be kept out of the conversation. By the same token, beware of the psychic who asks personal questions right off the bat. A reputable medium will not ask questions; she or he will make statements that the sitter can either accept or deny. A number of Spiritualist mediums have thrived on seemingly innocent questions that supplied them with the bulk of their "psychic information." Such deceit is made possible only with the collaboration of the naive sitter, of course. A sitter who does not answer leading questions is not likely to be deceived.

Once the sitting begins (most psychic readers or mediums will give their clients a sign that they are getting "into" the sitting), full attention should be paid to everything that is coming from the lips of the psychic. If the reader is merely a clairvoyant, using personal psychic abilities to give the reading, information will be coming forth almost immediately. If the psychic is of the Spiritualist persuasion, alleged communications from spirits may be supplying the medium with information he or she gives to the sitter. In the case of trance mediums, a control will first speak through the entranced medium, announcing himself or herself, and frequently this announcement will be followed by discarnates speaking directly with the sitter through the medium. It is permissible for the sitter to reply to the discarnates. When the psychic practitioner speaks as herself or himself, giving information obtained through ESP, the sitter need only take notice. At times, the medium may ask the sitter to confirm or deny a statement made. If so, it is quite sufficient to say yes, no, or maybe. Any further elaboration while the sitting is still in progress is self-defeating. Once the sitting has been concluded, however, the sitter should feel free to comment upon the medium's accuracy or inaccuracy. But even then the sitter should keep in mind the possibility that he may wish to return for another session at some future date. Consequently, the information disclosed by the psychic practitioner at this first meeting and confirmed by the sitter might become a repetitive element the next time, in which case it would no longer have any evidential value whatsoever. Therefore, when additional sittings are contemplated by the client, the client should be sparing in his or her use of words and cautious in his or her confirmation. In reassuring the medium that he or she has done a good job, the client must avoid furnishing the medium with information that he or she could use consciously or unconsciously in future sittings. The medium does not necessarily use such information fraudulently, but his or her unconscious mind may pick up information that will reappear on future occasions.

At times, a psychic may be unable to make the necessary contact with the sitter, perhaps because a sitter is too "cold"—has knowingly or unknowingly put up a defensive shield—or because of personal circumstances concerning the medium. In order not to disappoint the sitter, the medium will request an object belonging to the client to use as an inducing agent so that he or she can get into the vibration of the sitter. Through psychometry, the ball gets rolling, so to speak, and the reading proceeds. Some mediums, of course, are strictly psychometrists and can only interpret impressions gained by touching objects.

Psychic practitioners run the gamut from excellent and evidential to bad, just as other human beings vary greatly in their qualities. A client has the right to demand a certain level of performance if a professional is being paid for a sitting. A client should not be satisfied with generalities, well-meaning pastoral advice, and statements about dead relatives that are so vague that they could apply to anyone. In particular, names, or at least initials, of individuals referred to by the medium should be demanded; specific circumstances and detailed descriptions of events alluded to should be requested; and in general, a channeling of the medium's abilities toward a reasonably accurate description of events or persons should be expected. The late Eileen Garrett, probably one of the world's greatest mediums, was extremely adamant about poor performance by "sloppy" mediums. She always insisted that a medium come up with dates and names, detailed circumstances, and evidential material each time out. Her own training by the late Dr. Hewitt Mackenzie of the British College of Psychic Studies made her into the great, evidential medium she became, and she wanted no less from her colleagues in the field.

Uninitiated sitters sometimes have strange ideas regarding fees for psychic work. Some even think that payment for unsuccessful sittings is not called for. I recall that motion-picture actress Miriam Hopkins once asked the late Betty Ritter to come to her house for a reading. Hopkins herself was highly psychic, and she was also very difficult to get along with at times. I do not know what happened between the two women, but apparently Hopkins was not altogether satisfied with Ritter's reading and refused to pay. When I discovered this, I took into account the work put in by Ritter and the financial status of Hopkins and asked Hopkins to pay Ritter for her time whether she liked the reading or not. In some states, for legal reasons, psychic practitioners do not charge for their work per se but for the time given to a client. After all, a medical doctor does not charge for successful healing but only for time, knowledge, and effort. If the doctor fails, the patient doesn't get the money back.

What, then, is a proper fee? The answer will depend on the nature of the sitting. Some people prefer to go to a public sitting, in a Spiritualist church or other accessible place, in which anywhere from five to fifty people are read individually and publicly. Sometimes, especially when a medium is well known, as many as one thousand people will fill a major concert hall for the sole purpose of receiving messages from their loved ones on the other side of life. In these public sittings, a modest contribution of between five and ten dollars is standard nowadays. Although the contribution is called a "free will offering," one is expected to pay.

Private bookings run anywhere from fifty dollars to five hundred dollars, depending on the medium. Most reputable mediums who have become established through their evidential performance will charge between fifty and one hundred dollars for a sitting, but some will charge more. Many little-known mediums of good quality will give sittings for as little as twenty dollars.

What is considered good evidence, and what is not? When a psychic reader whom you have just met for the first time tells you some pertinent facts about your own past or present, including names, dates, and situations, and if the majority of the statements are accurate, then it stands to reason that the reader's statements about your future may also turn out to be accurate. Predictions concerning well-known people or those in the limelight of public attention cannot be taken seriously unless they are very specific. The prediction that an elderly celebrity may die within the following year is not a psychic prediction but a good guess, considering the person's age. The prediction that someone may try to shoot the president of the United States isn't psychic either; the president is a very likely target for a potential assassin, especially in times of stress. On the other hand, predictions concerning private individuals who are not in the public eye are more likely to be evidential, especially if they are precise and contain names and dates. I have described some of these amazing predictions with individual practitioners later in this book.

Evidence, then, consists of a fair percentage of hits, detailed material that comes true, without intensive questioning on the part of the medium. Do not expect a professional psychic to be good each time out or to be equally as good with your friend as with you. A number of factors affect each reading, and conditions may cause results to vary a great deal. Mediums, on the other hand, should know better than to give sittings when they are physically low or emotionally disturbed.

You have only to open some of the popular magazines devoted to psychic phenomena and the occult in general to see the great range of practitioners available to the public. The advertising matter appearing in such magazines as *Fate* shows how many kinds of individuals vie for the consumer's dollar in this field. Many of these ads may be legitimate, but there are such pearls as these: "Are you occult? Would you like to find out? For free lesson send postcard to . . . ," and "Are you unlucky? The girl whose dreams never come true? The man success passes by? Now you can do something about it! This age old symbol of Irish luck, the lucky leprechaun, cast in the original good luck mold from gleaming solid silver or gold can now be yours." How can you resist an ad reading, "You can use spiritual power and gain money," or "I dare you to be great. Do you want money, love, happiness, peace and success in special goals?" All you have to do is buy a certain book. "Now, right at home you can learn how to become a witch!" (Yes! I want to be a genuine witch. Send me lesson 1 of *You Can Become a Witch*, for which I enclose $4.95.) I especially like these: "Master your life. Call on secret guardians, their powers and the ancient Solomonic rite known by the Old Ones." "Giant power prayer. Send $5.00 for magic power prayer and blessed lucky numbers. Act now. Be surprised!"

Then there are advertisers who will answer three questions for two or three dollars, by mail of course; the self-appointed bishops of one-man or one-woman churches; the mysterious orders of this and that, which exist only in the fertile imaginations of the advertisers. Not all of these advertisements appear in *Fate* magazine, to be sure, but wherever such people look for clientele, beware of them.

If your quest is not for a psychic reading but for something more than that, such as a so-called life reading, you should realize that there was only one Edgar Cayce, and as yet no one has come forward to equal his feats. Life readings offered by a number of well-meaning and some not-so-well-meaning individuals, at fees ranging from twenty dollars to one hundred dollars, are largely fantasies that cannot be checked out for veracity. Sooner or later anyone with genuine memories of a previous life will come to realize his or her previous existence through flashes of memory, recurrent dreams, or some form of déjà vu. Deliberately seeking out one's former lives, just out of curiosity, invites delusion. Occasionally, reputable mediums may obtain flashes of information having to do with the previous lifetimes of a sitter. Ethel Johnson Meyers, one of the most reputable mediums around, frequently tells a sitter what he or she did in an earlier lifetime or why he or she is going through certain difficulties in this one. I don't doubt Meyers's sincerity, nor the source of her information, but it is always difficult to prove such statements, in the accepted scientific sense, unless actual names, dates, and situations that can be checked out are revealed.

Don't ask a medium to get in touch with a dead relative or to induce communications, because you will either fail or fall victim to fraud. If a discarnate wishes to communicate with you for good reasons, he or she will find a way to get through to you. Reasons include the need to demonstrate continued existence in another dimension, unfinished business on the earth plane, or a state of difficulty in your own life that the discarnate relative or friend wishes to help you with. The best hope for such a contact is to sit with a competent psychic and open yourself up to whatever or whoever might "come through." A psychic reading is not a telephone communication. You cannot dial the person to whom you wish to speak, and you cannot make demands other than to be given a reading containing as much identification and evidential material as the medium is capable of giving.

Another common misconception concerns the ability of the dead to instruct the living in matters of superior knowledge. While it is true that discarnate relatives frequently guide those on the earth plane, they do so without breaking any of the laws of nature and are in fact only helping the living people help themselves. Then, too, it should be realized that humans who pass into the next dimension after physical death do not automatically acquire some superior spiritual or other knowledge but that they are simply people existing in a dimension in which thought is the only reality. They, too, must learn to live in the new dimension and acquire knowledge that was denied them in their earthly existence. To assume that the spirit person has vastly superior foreknowledge is to delude oneself; on occasion, discarnates are permitted to divulge bits and pieces of information that might prove helpful to the person on the earth plane, but the communication is always done in accordance with universal law and under the control of the spirit guide supervising the communication. We should realize that the spiritual dimension is as subject to strict laws and natural conditions as is the denser physical dimension in which we presently exist.

A reputable psychic will give honest readings without editing anything, whether the message is good or bad and even if it warns of danger of imminent death. No knowledge should be held back if the medium is truly an intermediary and nothing more. However, the medium should give negative messages in a cautious and soothing way, always leaving the door open to the possibility of error or misinterpretation. In this manner, the dire warning becomes merely a bit of foreknowledge with which the sitter is being armed rather than the unfailing sword of Damocles hanging overhead about which he or she cannot do anything. Sitters should never ask professional psychics whether they see such and such in the future or what they think about such and such a person. By mentioning events, specific persons, or some special characteristic of themselves and expecting the psychics to render opinions, the sitters are in fact only looking for emotional crutches. Such crutches are more properly found among ministers and psychologists, not mediums. If, however, a sitter is anxious about a certain aspect of his or her life, the sitter may put the question in general terms, without divulging any detail, hoping that the psychic reader will come up with something that fits the situation. If the psychic does, the sitter should take into account the possibility of some thought reading entering the result, meaning that the psychic may very well pick up on the sitter's own thoughts and intermingle them with genuine psychic material. In any event, living one's life relying upon the opinions and predictions of psychic individuals is a poor way of spending one's time. Ultimately, all decisions rest with us, opportunities being thrust at us by fate. We are free to act, free to accept, reject, or ignore conditions around us; and while we seek the professional services of psychic practitioners, we should not abdicate our decision-making powers to them under any circumstances. If the majority of psychic professionals were infallible, then sitters consulting a number of such practitioners should obtain parallel readings. But they do not. Frequently, readings differ or give totally opposite material. Yet there are many instances on record in which the same information was obtained from a variety of psychic professionals. I myself have obtained proof of the veracity of a number of such statements from half a dozen professional psychics who knew nothing of each other or of me. On the whole, however, readings are affected by the personal conditions of both sitter and psychic at the time of the reading, interpretations, prejudices, and other as yet not fully understood elements. Thus if the same sitter consults a variety of readers, the results will never be 100 percent identical. Ultimately, psychic readings help you to understand yourself better, give you an occasional glimpse of what lies ahead, and afford you the chance to be prepared for it when it comes. Psychic readings also support your convictions that life goes on beyond physical death and that those who have gone before you are indeed alive and well and able to communicate with you at certain times and under certain conditions. The psychic world, then, complements the material world, and the truly happy individual is one who lives his own life in a state of harmony, drawing on both sensory perceptions of the material world and extrasensory knowledge from the next state of existence.

3

How Accurate Are Psychics?

It was 10:00 A.M. on December 5, 1966. The telephone rang in my office on Riverside Drive.

"Hello," said the voice on the other end of the line. "I hope I'm not disturbing you."

"Not at all," I assured my caller. It was Betty Ritter, one of my favorite mediums and a good friend. Usually she had something of interest to tell me. I was all ears. But Betty only wanted to know when my next book was due. After we had chatted for a minute or so, she suddenly said, "Cathy will sell two paintings."

Cathy is my ex-wife. Betty knew she was a painter. But there had been no discussion of her work recently. Her last exhibit had been in September. Why all of a sudden this remark? Betty had no idea. It had just come to her and she felt compelled to tell me.

The following day there was a letter in the mail for my wife. A man who had read a story about her wanted to buy a painting. He later did.

The day after that, my wife's music teacher suddenly decided that he wanted one of her works. He bought one.

That's a prediction—one that comes true as made. No mind reading here, since Ritter had no access to the two prospective buyers. Their paths had not crossed hers.

The place was London. The date was September 13, 1964. Catherine and I sat across from a portly lady named Magdalene

Kelly in a tiny room at the headquarters of the London Spiritualist Association. Ten minutes earlier I had never heard of Mrs. Kelly, nor had Mrs. Kelly heard of us. To her, we were two strangers who had walked in from the street to have a routine reading. It was all part of her day.

"I see the map of Ireland all over you. . . . Ireland will be very important in your lives," she said. I smiled politely. I had no intention of going to Ireland, I was not doing anything having to do with the Irish. No doubt Kelly's ancestors were getting into the act, I thought. Later I learned that Kelly was Scottish.

About four months after this sitting, my literary agent suggested that I do a book about Ireland. I did. Literally, I was all over the map of Ireland to do my research during 1965 and 1966. The book, *The Lively Ghosts of Ireland*, was published on March 17, 1967. The cover had the map of Ireland on it.

That, too, was a prediction.

On March 11, 1966, we were riding through Connecticut after a hard day's psychic work in New Haven. Catherine was driving and Ethel Johnson Meyers was resting from her trance chores. Suddenly Ethel sat up and said, "Your manuscript . . . the one you're worried about . . . a man with a name like Markowich will help you."

Ethel knew that I had an unpublished novel I wanted to see published by the right kind of firm. But we had not talked about it lately.

I shrugged. I didn't know anyone with a name like that. But there was a Maxis, an editor my agent knew at one of the companies she dealt with. The next morning, we submitted the book to Maxis. He turned it down flat. I put the whole thing out of my mind. Ethel had been wrong.

Nine months later, in the middle of December, I submitted the manuscript to a major motion picture company. The executive I knew was on his way to Europe, so his right-hand man would read it. His name? Mankiewicz. Close enough, I thought. He liked the book.

That prediction certainly cannot be explained away by coincidence or so-called ordinary causes.

As the derivation of the word implies, *to predict* means to say something ahead of time. A prediction—as distinguished from a prophecy or a premonition—is a forthright statement from a psychic person concerning an event as yet in the future. If the event transpires and is verified, we have evidence that can be counted toward establishing the reality of this human phenomenon. There are several million such cases, and anyone who doubts the possibility of predictions need only study the considerable documented literature on the subject.

On the face of it, the accurate foretelling of the future should not be possible. How can an event that has not yet happened or even *begun* to develop be known to someone ahead of time? Some predictions are of events that occur the next day; others occur years later. Unless we are willing to reexamine the very nature of "time," these things cannot be accounted for.

Currently, two kinds of researchers are dealing with psychic phenomena involving prediction. One group is trying desperately to punch holes in as many cases as possible, leaving the small number of "inexplicable" cases unattended "for the present." To them, any proof that a preordained fate exists would be unacceptable, no matter how convincing. They are not willing to follow the evidence wherever it leads them.

The other group of researchers is willing to unlearn anything traditional and accept new thoughts, regardless of philosophical consequences. All they ask is that the evidence be properly presented. I am among them. I've examined a good deal of evidence, though far more evidence exists than I will ever have access to.

Predictions can be proved. They are real. Not all predictions are perfect. Nothing involving human observation and interpretation is. Not all medical men are knowledgeable or honest. There are crooked lawyers, stupid teachers, lousy carpenters. I have decided to sift the true from the false and present my own version of the case for the reality of prediction.

A personal prediction has meaning to only a limited number of people, usually the one to whom it is given and at most to his or her family. Thus, confirmation is not so readily available as it is when a predicted world event occurs. But personal predictions can be more valuable to psychic research for the very reason that the element of general knowledge is absent.

When I first started to investigate personal predictions—both those made to me and those made to others but known to me—I naturally expected a certain number of failures. Anything involving human ability is bound to be imperfect. Persons who hold up the failures of predictions to materialize as proof of their fallacy are reminded that *any* prediction's coming true is a surprise if we use the old-fashioned laws of probability as a measuring stick. By those standards, if 98 percent of all of the predictions that are made were tabulated and found to be incorrect and 2 percent were found to be correct, that would be 2 percent too many. The proven reality of even 2 percent of all predictions would pose a challenge to the scientific community that could not be ignored. If predictions can come true at all, something is lacking in the law of cause and effect, something requiring further study and, ultimately, a reevaluation of that law.

It is regrettable that not all of the predictions that are properly made by qualified psychics come true. Failures can be ascribed to a number of outside factors, notably human failure to evaluate properly, misunderstanding of symbols, and wishful thinking and consequent embroidery of material.

Personal predictions are made by people in all walks of life, not just by professional clairvoyants and mediums. Some of these impressions of future events come while the psychic person is awake, some while he or she is in the dream state, when the bounds between the conscious and the unconscious mind are looser and the door to perception is ajar. Some persons are most receptive to psychic messages in the period just before sleep or just after awakening, when the physical and mental responses to being awake are not yet clearly defined. Other persons are most receptive when they are extremely tired.

A person who is alert and fully occupied is less likely to receive psychic material. However, flash impressions can cut through, especially when danger to oneself or to a loved one is involved.

Mrs. W., a young housewife in Ontario, California, was looking for a job. During that period, she had a dream in which she was holding two leopardlike cats on a leash. They were black cats with white spots. She could not fathom the meaning of this odd dream, but three days later she went for a job interview with a company whose letterhead showed two black leopardlike cats with white spots, identical with the dream impression!

Mrs. W. has often used her psychic talents to help others. When a friend, Mary S., informed her that she was going to spend a weekend in Las Vegas, Mrs. W. felt compelled to warn her that she would lose all her money there except for a few dollars—less than four—and that it was important for her to keep a ten-dollar bill in the back of her wallet toward that event. She would need that "nest egg," Mrs. W. explained to her startled friend, because she would have car trouble on the way home. Mrs. S. went to Las Vegas, lost all her ready cash except for four dollars, and on her way back to Los Angeles had to have her car repaired after sand got in the motor.

In Toronto, Canada, a professional tea-leaf reader named Jean Fraser, aged seventy-one, was in trouble with the police for fortune-telling. Three policewomen had consulted her and then arrested her. When she was brought before a magistrate, the question of accuracy arose, for, after all, one cannot accuse someone who has told the truth of fraud.

Fraser had told one of the policewomen that she came from a family of three and that she would be married in April of that year on a day with a two in it. This was correct; she was one of three children and did marry on April 28 of that year. Since Fraser had also given the other two policewomen correct readings, the case was dismissed.

The prediction of an event that was to happen at a distance in space rather than in time is contained in the case of a young girl reported by Lester David in *Science & Mechanics*: The girl was on an outing with two cousins when rain forced them to take shelter. Suddenly, she saw and heard a white car skid on the pavement somewhere in the distance, saw the car hit a bridge abutment, jump a creek, and hit a tree. She was sure that an accident had occurred and that someone was hurt. Later that day, confirmation came. The accident had happened exactly as she had seen it at a spot many miles away.

I met Trixie Allingham, one of the nicest professional mediums I've ever known, in London, where she then worked with the renowned College of Psychic Science. A Mr. Richardson came to see Trixie for a sitting, for he had heard of her ability. Among other things, Trixie told him of a triptych consisting of three pictures with foreign writing underneath and of two dolls that would be linked with him. Richardson laughed at these statements, disclaiming any knowledge of such objects. When he returned home several hours later, however, he found to his amazement that a cousin of his had arrived unexpectedly from Egypt. Among the objects that he had brought along were a triptych and two dolls, which he presented to Richardson.

In 1956, Trixie gave a reading to a Miss Savage, who then lived in London. Trixie told Miss Savage that she would change jobs and as a consequence would have to move to Tunbridge Wells. Miss Savage demurred, saying that she had a good job as matron in a children's home and that she wouldn't dream of leaving London. The prophecy was forgotten, and Savage continued on her job. Ten years later, she accepted another position—in Tunbridge Wells, where she now lives.

Ethel Johnson Meyers is well known to my readers because she was one of the two trance mediums—the other was Sybil Leek—with whom I worked regularly when investigating haunted houses and ghosts. There is no denying that Ethel, a voice teacher by profession, was working at her best when she was "somebody else," that is, taken over by an entity that was earthbound in a haunted house. But Ethel, in a quiet way, was also a clairvoyant of renown.

I first met Ethel in 1947 during study sessions of the Association for Research and Enlightenment, better known as the Cayce Foundation. Ethel has given me many spontaneous predictions, sometimes at odd moments. Early in 1955, in the course of a long reading, Ethel mentioned a star, Christmas, and wise men. It was not until 1965, ten years later, that I wrote *Star in the East,* which deals with Christmas and the story of the Wise Men.

Later on, in June 1955, Ethel predicted that I would write three books—I have since surpassed that number by over one hundred, but in 1955 not even *one* book was likely. The first three books that I wrote were, in a way, a unit, since they concerned ghostly happenings in the United States in which Ethel was the medium whereas my next book did not.

In the same 1955 session, a man named Bailey was mentioned. I did not meet Mel Bailey until 1966, when he became important in my career as the executive producer of a television show that I was preparing.

"My experiences with Mrs. Ethel Meyers have never ceased to amaze me," writes Carol I., a woman who consulted Ethel on a number of occasions. On December 23, 1966, Carol was told that her career modeling would be a disappointment but that in February 1967 she would become involved in motion pictures and as a result would be doing a great deal of photography. At the time, none of these developments were likely. Nevertheless, on February 13, 1967, Carol confirmed that the predictions had happened.

Mr. and Mrs. A. were not given to belief in the occult. Mr. A. was an executive in a chemical manufacturing business. Mrs. A. had heard of Ethel's work in ESP; and in April 1966, without her husband, she came to consult her for a "general reading." To induce some psychic material, Mrs. A. gave Ethel a watch to hold and through psychometry was able to make contact with the couple's respective psychic auras.

Instantly Ethel described them being on a vacation and having a marvelous time but said that the husband would become impatient to get back to town. This was not at all likely, Mrs. A. thought, for she knew that her husband never let business matters interfere with his enjoyment of a vacation. But she listened politely as Ethel continued with her predictions.

"On the eighteenth of May 1966, your husband will be offered a higher position with his present company. Even though he joined the company only recently, he already feels stagnant in his job." Mrs. A. was surprised. It was true that her husband had joined the company only the previous September. A change in position after so short a period seemed unlikely to her.

"Furthermore," Ethel continued, "on May 19, the following day, your husband will get a telephone call from the company he was with until recently, asking him to go back and offering a very good position. As if that were not enough, the week of May 20 he will get still another call about a further advancement of his career." All three calls would come unsolicited and spontaneously, she added.

"I must say that at this point my husband had no intentions of changing jobs, nor did he have any offers or even hints of such," Mrs. A. states in a letter confirming these facts. But a month later, things began to happen in the life of the As. An executive in the company left unexpectedly on May 16, and on May 18 the president of the company offered Mr. A. the position. A. gladly accepted the advancement. But the following day—May 19, as predicted—A.'s former employer telephoned to offer him an important position with the company if he would return. A. decided to stall. He told his former employer he was just going on vacation and would see him after his return in June.

On later checking her notes, Mrs. A. found to her amazement that her husband had used the identical words Ethel Meyers had predicted he would use on that occasion!

During the week of May 20, the executive who had suddenly left A.'s company and whose position A. now held got in touch with him. Would he have lunch with him?

In the business world, having lunch means discussing business. The matter at hand was a suggestion that A. desert the company and join the gentleman in his new place at a great increase in prestige and salary—at triple his present salary, in fact. Again A. decided to mull things over and asked for time. He was about to go on vacation and would make a decision upon his return.

At this point, Mrs. A. decided to go back to Ethel and see what the outcome of all this would be. So much of the predicted material had turned out to be right that perhaps Ethel could also supply the clues to the solution. Ethel predicted that A. would leave his current company and take one of the two other offers.

When the couple went on vacation, Mrs. A. noticed that her husband, for the first time, was restless and eager to get back to town, and the prediction to this effect came to mind. They went back to the city, and A. took the third offer, at three times his latest salary. On checking her notes, Mrs. A. noticed that that was exactly what Ethel had said he would get. Again she paid Ethel a visit.

"My husband has taken one of the two offers," she began,

but before she could go any further, Ethel interrupted her.

"Yes, the *third* offer. He has made the right decision. I knew he would."

I met the great medium Sybil Leek in New York in the mid-sixties. At that time she had some nine books to her credit, dealing with animal life, antiques, and other subjects. On June 13, 1966, Sybil warned me about my impending trip to Germany. I was due to lecture at Freiburg University on July 11, and nothing seemed to be amiss. Everything was well prepared, I was most welcome, and I saw no reason to postpone the trip. But Sybil foresaw my getting caught in "some strange political web when in Germany" around the middle of July.

It turned out to be only too true. A local psychic researcher took umbrage at my lecture topic regarding proof of survival (and perhaps at the huge turnout I had at my lecture) and managed to stir up considerable trouble for me. From planted heckling and personal criticism down to newspaper stories about my appearance, I was indeed caught in a strange web of intrigue!

On July 14, 1966, Sybil wrote to me in Europe that she saw difficulties and unpredictable events cropping up. She was right. That week, my father was taken to the hospital and passed away ten days later. We had to return two days earlier than planned and found ourselves in the midst of a number of pressing problems. Also, every conference I had planned for the period went badly. It was as if I had run into a wall of indifference.

In September of the same year, Sybil foresaw an "unexpected largesse" for me "as a result of past hard work." She continued her prediction with the remark that "some hidden asset soon bears fruit . . . and it is linked with the occult." On September 29, I received a letter concerning work I had done on a television series ten years before, and as a result, I was able to cash in on "hidden assets" and "past hard work," just as Sybil had said I would.

On November 2, 1966, Sybil wrote that in February 1967, a contract for *Psychic Investigator* (which she thought was a book title) would come through. Unbeknownst to her, the title of the television series I had worked on ten years before and which was now being considered was *Psychic Investigator.*

On January 12, 1967, Sybil reported a strange semitrance experience that she felt had some significance for me. It was the second time that she had "seen" this scene, the first time having been about two weeks earlier. At that time she had reported it to me on the telephone. I merely thanked her without further comment. The scene that Sybil Leek described was on the Bath road in England. Horses and a carriage draw up, the door opens, and inside is a dead man dressed in clothes of the Charles II period.

At the time, Sybil did not know that such an event had actually taken place in the seventeenth century and that it involved an ancestor of the present marquess of Bath. It was one of the stories in a motion picture that Sybil and I had been discussing but had not yet begun filming. It is a moot question whether Sybil was experiencing retrocognition of the actual event or precognition of our film depiction of the event or both.

Probably the psychic who was best able to help me with my study of the percentage of predictions documented and proven correct was the late Betty Ritter, with whom I started working in the 1940s.

On May 13, 1961, Betty mentioned that a Harry and a Peter Brown would assume importance in my life. At the time, the names meant nothing to me. However, in the spring of 1963, I met a Harry H., and we did have a certain business relationship. Peter Brown came into my life at the end of 1965, and we became involved in a project of some importance.

At the same reading, I was told that L.A. was "in trouble" and that I should keep my fingers crossed, for something about to happen; and L. was smoking a peace pipe and holding up a horseshoe while E. was negotiating. None of this made any sense to me until the end of 1966, when there was indeed trouble in L.A. (Los Angeles) over a television series that I had created and that L. had appropriated and tried to sell to E. But I was offered half of the proceeds (the horseshoe meaning money) if I'd smoke the peace pipe and negotiate with E., which I did.

It appears that certain events are formulated or shaped by destiny in a manner that we still do not fully understand; we approach these events gradually, but a clairvoyant can somehow see the events approaching through the "surrounding mist." At first, the clairvoyant may see only an outline, a silhouette; but as time (as we know it) goes on, the picture becomes clearer, and eventually he or she can make out more and more details.

On March 4, 1962, when the idea of motion pictures was farthest from my thoughts, Betty first saw me involved in movies. It was just a thought, "motion pictures," nothing more.

Even the best clairvoyants—and Betty was among them—cannot be relied upon when it comes to dates. What they may see as imminent may not come to pass for years; and by the time the event does occur, one may have forgotten about the prediction. I think this time factor is one of the reasons that the average person considers the accuracy of predictions close to nil. But if we eliminate the artificial time barriers, we suddenly find that a very high percentage of predictions are indeed accurate. For example, on February 7, 1964, Betty described a vision concerning my future work in which she saw the letter *A* and *B* turn into a *P*; the vision had something to do, she felt, with a screen. She did not give a date for this occurrence. In January 1967, I found myself discussing some films with American Broadcasting–Paramount (AB–P).

In a sitting on July 11, 1964, Betty had "seen" two people getting together in the future to discuss a motion picture. I was one, and the other was a person with the initial *K.* The discussion would be about a book, to use "a little of this and that" from it for the picture, and a trip to Europe would be necessary.

Occasionally, Betty got a visual impression in the form of a picture or drawing. Such was the case in the following week, on July 18, 1964, when she added to the prediction of July 11 that there would be a "survey" and that she saw a radiant star or sun symbol and the letter *L*. It made absolutely no sense to me.

As it turned out, in the fall of 1966 I did have discussions with a man whose name begins with a K. And I made a survey trip to London for Columbia Pictures, whose trademark is a figure holding a radiant torch.

After this sitting, my wife and I went to Europe to do research for one of my books, and several months passed. On our return I was too busy writing to find the time for a sitting. We saw Betty only sporadically because I was out of town a great deal; the only knowledge that she could have had of my activities would have been from my books and radio and television interviews.

I never discussed my affairs with Betty. Unfortunately, many a worried individual turns a simple psychic into a psychoanalyst or a marriage counselor, a role for which most psychics have no talent. To ask a medium what she "gets" about certain people or conditions is begging the issue. It is also furnishing information that would invalidate the evidence of genuine prediction. I only listen, never question.

Although I never commented on the material that she gave me in previous sessions, Betty predicted situations, conditions, names of individuals I would deal with, and even the outcomes, each time in exactly the same words and images, although as much as a year may have elapsed between sittings. Considering that she did not keep notes of her predictions, that she never read my notes, and that my own thoughts were not turned to earlier predictions—plus the undeniable fact that she read for many people throughout the year—one cannot possibly ascribe Betty Ritter's consistency to fraud or coincidence.

For a period of two years (1960 and 1961), I kept a record of the psychics who read for me. My purpose was not to be able to tally the percentage of correct predictions but to determine how often different psychics made the same predictions. It stands to reason that if a statement is correct, more than one medium should be able to get its component facts. If a large number of receivers tune in to a radio program at the same time, some will get the program, and others will not. Powerful receivers will get it clearly; others, less clearly; and some may not get it at all because of malfunction, distance, or atmospheric conditions. I decided that I would be satisfied if a portion of the psychics whom I consulted made the same predictions.

Obviously, if only two mediums are used for a reading and both give different material, it cannot be said that one is wrong and the other is right. Both may be right; or both, wrong. If half a dozen or more psychics read the same person, however, a certain percentage of the facts should match, even accounting for human failure and loss in transmission from *there* to *here*.

My method differs considerably from pure laboratory experiments because I go into the field for spontaneous phenomena—in this instance, readings by psychic persons of the same subject, me. But after I collect this spontaneous material, I analyze it according to orthodox statistical methods. Such methods may not be the answer entirely, for statistics can mislead. Then again, a psychic reading is not the spontaneous phenomenon that a haunting or a psychic manifestation is, since my requesting the reading introduces an element of experimentation. But the medium's lack of knowledge of my background and the irregularity with which I seek out these readings would, in my opinion, bring a reading within the framework of what is generally called spontaneous phenomena in parapsychology.

I should like to point out that the often-mentioned idea of mind reading, that the reader taps the subject's conscious and unconscious mind, deserves some healthy skepticism. For one thing, no one has ever even proved conclusively that one person can really read the mind of another. Telepathy exists, but only between two individuals well attuned to each other. The readings given by a medium to a stranger cannot be explained by telepathy.

If I were to confront a psychic reader when I had certain names and facts clearly in mind, perhaps the reader could pick up on my thoughts. But the idea that the reader can dig out of the sitter's unconscious mind names and facts long forgotten or submerged seems to me rather farfetched, and it does a disservice to the amazing ability of some good psychics to come up with pertinent material. In addition, one must consider that in many instances the unconscious mind does not yet have the information and thus cannot be a source.

I do, however, think that a person is surrounded by a magnetic field that extends beyond his physical body and that this field contains certain impulses pertaining to both past and future. It may be that some of these impulses contribute to the knowledge gained by a psychic reader, but there are many cases where other explanations are on the whole more logical and preferable. Some mediums will tell a subject that their information is given to them by discarnates, relatives, controls, or others and that they are merely the channels through which the information flows. This explanation, of course, relieves them of responsibility for the truth of the material. Others make no such claims but ascribe the knowledge they convey to their own ESP talents.

It is a moot point whether the medium is self-made or is helped by unseen hands from beyond the veil: mediumship still involves psychic talents and the ability to obtain information by other means than the five senses.

To the reincarnation theorists this presents no problem: at birth we are given a sort of ID card—an identity stamp already containing our life pattern from beginning to end. We ourselves may not be privileged to read it, but the psychic person can interpret it for our benefit.

Some of these life readers are enormous frauds, usually imitators of the great psychic Edgar Cayce. But there are honest mediums who simply sense future events in a kind of visionary flash. I have always felt that readings having to do with future events tend to be genuine, and they are certainly capable of verification, while those having to do with previous incarnations tend to be fanciful and rarely borne out by proof. I am still seeking a life-reading medium who can give a sitter a list of his or her past incarnations and have them verified scientifically as to names, dates, and circumstances. No doubt such cases exist, but they are yet to be discovered amid the fakery.

My record of the psychics that I consulted in 1960 and 1961 contains the following information:

General information
Number of psychics consulted: 6
Total number of consultations: 10
Sex of psychics: Female
Age group: Middle-aged and older
Health: Good

Number of recurrences of certain letters or words across predictions
J: 5
F, M: 4
A, G, doctor, John, W: 3
*Max, Robert, H, E, B, William, George, Elizabeth, Grace, Charles,
    R, Virginia, S, Harry:* 2
Other: 1

Matching predictions

Max: Betty Ritter, July 18, 1960; Carolyn Chapman, November 3, 1960

Robert: Betty Ritter, October 4, 1960; Carolyn Chapman, November 3, 1960

Doctor: "Titian," February 27, 1960; Betty Ritter, July 18, 1960, and October 4, 1960

R: Laurette, May 21, 1957; Betty Ritter, July 18, 1960; "Jesse," January 26, 1961

M: "Titian," February 27, 1960; Laurette, July 7, 1960; Betty Ritter, July 18, 1960; "Jesse," January 26, 1961

These examples will suffice to make my point, that correspondences do occur and that they are more frequent when the predictions involve a single letter and less frequent when they involve an entire word. The psychics tested did not know each other or even know of each other.

Genuine mediums will be consistent without even trying. A professional reader who sees hundreds of people every month cannot possibly keep mental track of every detail of his or her readings. The fakers keep index-card files, like those discovered in some of the American Spiritualist camps a few years ago, and exchange information on "steady" customers.

I have never seen a medium take notes while reading for me. Betty Ritter, the only psychic I know who used pencil and paper, wrote down letters and words impressed upon her and handed me the notes at the end of the session. I would not permit the taking of notes by anyone but myself. There is no way a genuine psychic can make a record of his or her reading. I look for such devices as tape recorders and have never found evidence that one was used in my presence.

Thus, it boils down to this: if a medium is consistent over a long period of time, and if this consistency covers a number of instances not easily remembered, it must be assumed that the medium is giving an authentic reading in each instance, that the source of this paranormal information, whatever it may be, is repeating the material because it is still correct!

No genuine medium will predict exact time; in fact, they will freely admit that telling events beforehand is far easier than pinning them down to a date, because in the psychic world, time as we know it does not exist. Thus, a prediction may take some earth time to materialize. The psychic, or another psychic perhaps, may give the same prediction again, since the time for its fulfillment has not yet arrived.

The impatient may find this hard to take, but the fact is that an impressive number of predictions made to me have eventually come true. Sometimes, especially when pressed, a medium will give the wrong date, but otherwise the event depicted occurs as described. This has happened to me in a number of instances and proves, to me at least, that the time element cannot be quite what we think it is, that it has a trickiness we are not yet fully cognizant of. Perhaps emotional and developmental factors have some influence on the timing of events—time having no absolute dimension but being a secondary factor that depends on both immaterial and personal influences.

Betty Ritter, at the time, was astonishingly correct. Some of the names or initials that she saw connected with my life were in her readings for several years. Some became significant in the material world, some have not.

An important point to remember is that certain elements of chance must be considered. Thus, if a reader says that you will have some business with a John or a Charles, chances are that you will because of the great number of people named John or Charles in this world. It is only when the predicted material is *specific* regarding time, space, or circumstances that we consider it likely to come to pass.

Channeling and Past Lives

Until a few years ago, channeling meant very little to the average esoteric seeker and nothing at all to the uncommitted outsider. The term *past lives* conveyed only some vague idea of previous existences until a respectable parapsychologist, Dr. Ian Stevenson, of the medical department at the University of Charlottesville, came out with strong and convincing evidence that reincarnation did in fact exist. Past lives then acquired the aura of scientific possibility and could be discussed openly among researchers in parapsychology. Channeling and reincarnation are not really closely related—after all, one deals with communications by some spiritual entity eager to use the human channel and the other with an individual's past lifetimes and experiences—but both, unfortunately, are sometimes invoked as a means of deception or self-delusion.

Let us deal with the channeling phenomenon first. Ever since I began to work in the field now called parapsychology, going back at least thirty years, I have been familiar with trance mediumship—in technical terms, dissociation of personality. When the medium is in a trance, an allegedly exterior or foreign personality uses the physical body, or "apparatus," of the medium to speak to the living.

In experimental studies of trance mediumship, the validity of the results will depend on the particular circumstances, such as background and education of the medium, test conditions, and supervision. Some researchers reject any notion that dead people speak through the living, regardless of evidence that points in that direction. Other researchers, including myself, interpret the authenticity of such phenomena strictly on the basis of results. If the material obtained through a trance medium is later verified, if it was unknown or inaccessible to the medium at the time of the experiment, and if it is sufficiently precise and detailed, any reasonable researcher will accept it as prima facie evidence in the absence of any strong evidence to the contrary.

Trance mediums are rare; why, I don't know, unless it is because the work is physically very strenuous. Nobody who has worked for many years with mediums will doubt that the medium undergoes extreme stress while working and that no actor can fake what transpires in front of the experienced researcher.

Ever since the nineteenth century, when spiritualism was in its heyday and took the place of parapsychology (with far more stringent sets of rules, to be sure), communication with the dead through the "instrument" of the trance medium has been studied, recorded, and published. Mainly in England and later in Boston and New York, the societies for psychical research took these experiments very seriously; it is a pity that so little work of this kind is done today under conditions eliminating fraud and deception of any kind.

While trance mediums tended to work more with private clients who were eager to hear from a loved one passed over (and sometimes did) or with the police on murder cases, to whom they provided valuable clues that were sometimes alleged to be from the victim directly (and sometimes with good results), most psychical researchers preferred to conduct their "tests" in the lab, under the postulated need of repeatability of the experiment before the phenomena would be scientifically accepted as genuine. It has always been my contention that repeatability of events involving ESP prove little, if anything, whereas competent, repeated, and careful observation of actual natural phenomena yields real clues and scientific data.

Then along came the channelers. On the surface, channelers looked and acted like trance mediums. They closed their eyes or rolled them dramatically before going into their particular state. Shortly thereafter a voice claiming to be someone other than the channeler would speak to the audience or client. With a trance medium, any researcher worth his scientific salt will demand identification of the alleged communicator, and he or she will usually get it fairly quickly if only in halting sentences. The researcher will then proceed to have a dialogue with the spirit entity, using the trance medium as a kind of telephone, and elicit as much detailed and personal information as he is able to in order to try to verify it later on. With the channeler, attempts at questioning these "entities" about personal background or even real names lead either to platitudes about the high level of their mission or to names and circumstances that cannot be verified.

Channeling has become a big business in the form of in-person seminars, where the faithful gather and, at a stiff price, are allowed to partake of the often questionable pearls of wisdom dropping from the lips of their channeler, as well as in audiotapes, books, magazines, and question-and-answer sessions where people seek the counsel of the channeling entity in solving their personal problems.

Perhaps the best-known channeler of them all is a woman named J. Z. Knight, who claims to be the spokeswoman (channel) for one Ramtha, whom she has characterized as a native of India who "lived thirty-five thousand years ago." Much of the style used by J.Z. in her Ramtha personality reminds one of Edgar Cayce, the granddaddy of trance communication, whom dozens upon dozens of would-be mediums have claimed as their inspiration, if not actual communicator. Just as with the Cayce material, eager groups of followers are gathering all of J.Z.'s readings so as to try to interpret them in such a way that they present a new, world-shaking approach to life.

It is my opinion that a healthy dose of skepticism is called for here. Let us assume for the moment that there really is an entity, a real person long deceased, who is speaking through J.Z., as happens with many reputable trance mediums. Would it not be sensible to establish that we are hearing from an "enlightened one" (as Ramtha repeatedly calls himself) who actually lived at one time or another in a place on this planet? Well, now, if we can't find his name listed in a directory, could he not enlighten us with specific, truly detailed knowledge of his time and place? Then we might get that certain feeling of authenticity that is the next best thing to actual proof.

Assuming for the moment that some very illustrious historical figures choose to manifest themselves through a channeler, would it not be likely that their personalities, their characters, their styles would somehow come through even in English?

I recall one of my earliest cases when the late medium and researcher Eileen Garrett accompanied me and the *Daily News* columnist Danton Walker to Walker's Revolutionary house in the Ramapo hills. There Eileen slipped into a deep trance and became the vehicle for a badly wounded soldier of Polish origin. The suffering man told us his terrible story—haltingly and piecemeal to be sure—including his name and the people he had been with. The authenticity of this voice was incredible; also, the name and circumstances checked out.

More recently, the clairvoyant and trance medium Yolana Lassaw, who often works with the police on unsolved crimes, accompanied a detective on the New York City police force and me to the site of a grisly murder that had not been solved. In a sudden, deep trance, Yolana, who knew absolutely nothing about the case or where we had taken her, spoke with the voice of the actual victim, figuratively pointing the finger at one of the suspects the police needed more information on!

On the other side of the coin, a woman who makes her living as a competent psychic reader assured me on a television program we shared that she was a channel for Saint Thomas Aquinas! And what did Saint Thomas have to say to us mortals? Pretty much of the same platitudes you get from most UFO contactees about the dear old space brothers who want to save the world from itself. Nothing about theology, deep thoughts, or history; this Saint Thomas was strictly unreal. But "I channel his essence," she intoned. Essence? Impersonating a saint?

Anyone with a gift for turning a clever phrase can claim to be channeling some exotic long-ago personality or "master." A very good book about channeling, by Jon Klimo, was recently published by Tarcher. In his foreword, the eminent psychical researcher Charles T. Tart makes no bones about the evidence (or lack of it) but suggests that the process of dealing with channeled material may help us know ourselves better. Perhaps it does.

Nothing in scientific research is an absolute. Not every "ascended master" is a figment of the imagination. But some kind of evidence should be required before the communication is accepted as genuine and as something external to the channeler or medium. Years ago, Ethel Johnson Meyers, who had worked with me on dozens of hauntings and brought through amazing evidence of a detailed nature, fell into deep trance during one of our many sittings. It so happened that the respected astrologer Charles Jayne was present. A personality that did not sound at all like Meyers spoke through her, greeting the astrologer and engaging in an hour of technical conversation about the exact positions and orbits of certain planets, including ones not yet discovered in our solar system. These planets were Jayne's specialty, so to speak; and after the session was over, Jayne went ahead and verified the material given to him by the communicator, who had freely given his name, Kamaraya, and the approximate time of his life on earth. Even that name is correct for the period and country of origin, something the medium could scarcely have known, her training having been in music.

Of course, few people will question the amazing material that was given in trance by Edgar Cayce, a photographer without any medical knowledge who prescribed valid cures and remedies for years. In the end, the proof of the pudding is in the eating: if the seeker wants sugar-coated platitudes, then indeed a channeler will do nicely. If the seeker is truly interested in communicating with an entity of higher intelligence, then he or she ought to be more sanguine about what represents the basic minimum of evidentiality in such communications.

First, the alleged communicator from the great beyond should identify himself or herself in some manner that is subject to verification—if not by individual name, then by authentic knowledge of the period and place that he or she claims to be from. In group sessions, of course, it may be more difficult to question the communicating entity. Still, those taking part in such sessions and plunking down good money for them should demand the right to do so.

Next, the nature of the material coming through the channeler should be examined critically. Channelers who claim only some vague long-dead master as their source will have to be questioned when they are "themselves" and not channeling. Any differences in style delivery, knowledge, and background between the channeler and the alleged communicator should be carefully examined.

Finally, it is just possible that some of the channeled pseudowisdom is helpful to the listeners. After all, Dianetics and est, though widely attacked as highly questionable, may have helped some people. But the occasional benefits of chan-

neling, when, for example, the material fits a preexisting need
that the participant does not want to address in a more conventional manner, should not be misinterpreted as validating
the method employed here. True deep trance is a genuine
psychic phenomenon, which, in the right hands, can be very
helpful both as a scientific tool of inquiry into the nature of
human beings and as a vital link between our world and the
next one. The large number of casual channelers are not a
part of this link.

The human mind, consciousness working through the physical brain while we are in the physical body, is capable of many
things that are not acceptable to old-fashioned empirical science. Tapping deeper levels of one's own consciousness or that
of others and deriving useful information from these levels is
not only possible but common.

Past lives is a term that has lately come into general usage;
a few years ago *reincarnation* was the term most commonly used
when speaking of the concept of being reborn in new bodies
to gain more experience in this world. In the East, the ideas
of karma and rebirth are old ones, and part of religious philosophy and culture. In the West, the study of the evidence for
reincarnation owes a great deal to Dr. Ian Stevenson of
Charlottesville, Virginia, and to his initial work, *Twenty Cases
Suggestive of Reincarnation.* Contrary to lay opinion, cases of reincarnation have occurred all over the world and not primarily
in India, where people "believe in reincarnation." But
Stevenson took the search out of metaphysics and into the
realm of scientific inquiry, where evidential standards must of
necessity be high. For a case to merit attention, detailed information of a previous existence, including names, dates, places,
and circumstances, must be provided. If the person claiming
to have had a previous life experience is shown to have had
no easy access to such information, and if that information
turns out to be correct, the case for reincarnation seems strong.
Personally, I add still another condition to proof of reincar-

nation: the person should not have any psychic ability, demonstrated either before or after the recall of reincarnation. If it can be shown that the person is psychic and has had psychic experiences before, the experience might be explained as communication by another entity.

Pamela Wollenberg, a young Illinois woman aged eighteen, sought me out because of recurrent dreams in which phrases were spoken to her by an entity that she "saw." The words were *Ruthven . . . Gowrie . . . Scotland 1600 . . . I leapt.* They made no sense to her, or for that matter, to me at the time. But subsequently I went to Scotland and started to investigate the matter. With considerable difficulty and diligent search, I finally found confirmation in an obscure locally published book about events in the highlands. The Ruthven family, whose "second," or noble, name was Gowrie, had been wiped out by the king in retaliation for an abduction that had taken place when he was but a lad. That was precisely in the year 1600, and Gowrie Castle was renamed Huntingtower Castle to wipe out even the name of the hated family.

Apparently, one of the young Gowrie women had been caught in a lover's room by her mother. She ran out of the room and jumped (leapt) from one of the two castle towers to the other, over the roof, and was thus able to escape her pursuing mother.

How was a simple eighteen-year-old girl in upstate Illinois to know this? Subsequent investigation through extended hypnotic regression established additional, detailed information, all of which I was later able to corroborate. I published the account as probably the best case for reincarnation that I had come across. Here, we had an "innocent" subject, Pamela, without a Scottish family background, without the appropriate education, and without access to the rare book I found in Scotland that gave me the key to the puzzle. Nobody in his right mind would accuse her of making up the story, and for what gain?

She was disturbed by all this and came to me for answers, which she did indeed get.

True past lives simply do not get recognized in detail in half-hour sessions with a reader. At best, a psychic may pick up some foreign elements from the sitter's own vibrations, for it appears that in all of us, without exception, past-life elements remain deeply imbedded to develop the personality through each successive incarnation. But these past elements are seldom detailed or even clear. Sometimes, in sudden flashes of memory, bits and pieces may emerge as in a déjà vu experience or in a recurrent dream. I have found, over the years, that these "bonus" memory bits in the present lifetime, come only from lives that were unfinished or unsettled in the past, perhaps to compensate for past deprivations and make this time around a little easier.

It is my conviction, based on years of active work in this field, that genuine reincarnation (past-life) memories make themselves known to the person sooner or later. The memories can either be ignored or pursued for clarification. Unquestionably, if one person reincarnates, then we all do. But only a comparatively few will remember, or be able to trace, their past lives in a way that is truly and fully convincing. Naturally, it may make a person feel very special to believe that he or she has spent an earlier existence in so romantic a place as Tibet or ancient Egypt—two favorites, by the way, of past-lives readers, along with the Holy Land at the time of Christ—but evidence and proof of the previous existence is another matter.

Just as with the channeling craze, the proof of authenticity lies in the specifics obtained through past-life regression. If a past-lives reader who practices his or her craft without benefit of deep regressive hypnosis comes up with substantial information that was previously unknown to both sitter and reader, well and good: the evidence speaks for itself. Rarely does this happen, however. Even in professionally induced hypnotic regression, which I have practiced for many years, only a few cases yield specifics that are capable of verification. Still, even a few cases tend to prove the reality of reincarnation.

Some otherwise honorable psychics mistake ESP information for genuine past-lives information. A psychic may pick up information about a client from the client's own unconscious or even from an ongoing spirit communication between the client and a discarnate entity and wrongly determine that the outside personality is the client in a previous lifetime. Unless careful research is done and certain test conditions are met, this kind of past-life work tends to be more imagination and suggestion than reality.

When an otherwise responsible person lays claim to being the reincarnation of a well-known historical figure, the proof is hard to come by. General George Patton repeatedly claimed that he was the reincarnation of Julius Caesar. His conviction was based in part on two elements: his feeling of familiarity with the part of France that had been Caesar's Gaul during the victorious Roman campaigns and an "inner voice" that guided him in his own campaigns there during World War II. The actor Ernest Borgnine believed that he was once Horatio at the Bridge, a legendary Roman hero whom we know only from the Latin classics and perhaps tradition rather than from hard historical facts.

Then there is still another category of past-life experiences: those in which a loved one or a relative who passed on years before returns. Mrs. Smith, of Oregon, assured me that her young son, aged seven, was really her first husband, dead fifteen years, who had come back to be with her. She was sure of it because of certain traits that the child possessed.

There *are*, of course, true cases of reincarnation: in nearly all of them, a person who died prematurely or tragically, returns relatively quickly and is recognized by someone in this life. Professor J. Banerjee reported the case of a young man in

India who insisted that he had a wife in a distant village. His parents eventually gave in and took the youth to the village that he had indicated. There, spontaneously, the youth made for the house that he claimed had been his and picked out a middle-aged woman in it by name, calling her his wife. In the ensuing session with Banerjee, the young man remembered so many accurate details about his alleged previous life that no doubt remained about the truth of his claims. That being India and not America, the parents agreed to the boy's taking up residence in the house with the family of his "former wife."

During World War II, an American GI who belonged to the advance guard of a military detachment entered a village in Belgium that he had never seen before. He and two buddies were simply looking for enemy stragglers. But as the three soldiers rounded a street corner, the GI in question made straight for a certain house. "My house, my house," he cried out, to the puzzlement of his comrades. Quickly, they entered the empty house and climbed the stairs to a second floor. At this point, the other two men started to question their comrade about his claim that the house was "his." Very agitated by now, the GI assured them that it was and that he had been a child in it when growing up "a long time ago." To prove his point, he told the others what they would find when they entered the upper story. He described a painting on the wall and all the furnishings in the room. Sure enough, when the men entered the room, it was exactly as he had said it would be. Coincidence? Surely not. Clairvoyance? ESP? Not likely. This GI had never shown the slightest psychic ability or interest before the incident, nor did he show any afterward.

Mrs. Frank lives in Macon, Georgia, with her husband. On a European trip as part of a group tour, the Franks found themselves in Florence for the first time. Suddenly, Mrs. Frank broke away from the group and insisted on walking through the elaborate iron gate of a palazzo across the street. Nothing could stop her; and for that matter, Mrs. Frank later described her experience as one of utter compulsion to enter that house at all costs because she had lived there in another lifetime. After she had gone into the building, she became calmer and then returned to the others. Apparently, there had been the need for her to become aware of and acknowledge her previous existence. The question remains: What made her come to Florence, to that house, in the first place?

When I was taping a pilot for a television program in Cleveland a few years ago, a group practicing "suggestive regression" under the control and guidance of a professional esoteric group leader caught my attention, and I proceeded to watch a session. Each of the dozen or so participants—all of them women, by the way—first went into a meditative state, presumably to tap the deeper levels of consciousness including past-life memories. Then each in turn spoke up and told me who she had been before. At least two of the women were sure that they had been Egyptians but the young Cleveland housewife who assured me that she had been Isadora Duncan, the dancer, in a previous life and that before that she had been the Queen of Sheba, Solomon's lover, particularly interested me. I realized that these were harmless fantasies—I knew of at least two other Isadora Duncans, in other cities—so I did not even attempt a serious investigation. But what little I saw and heard during the session made it clear to me that this nice group of women did not know very well at all the personalities they claimed to have been in their previous lives.

Anybody who wishes to believe that he or she has lived before as someone markedly different from (and probably more interesting than) his or her present self is of course welcome to that dream. I feel less charitable when I am confronted with an increasing number of casual practitioners giving past-life readings at a price. None of them use professional hypnotic regression to determine whether the sitter has, in fact, any memory of a previous incarnation; they prefer to do their readings intuitively, generally in terms that are incapable of true verification in books or records of any kind. In a particularly crass case, a woman who had been complaining of pains in her wrists and feet and who had not been able to get a medical explanation that satisfied her (such as a diagnosis of arthritis, rheumatism, or tension) consulted a young woman who did provide—and charge for—an answer that the woman found acceptable: the woman's pains were caused by her past-life crucifixion at the time of Christ. With that, the pains seemed to cease or at least to recede from the patient's attention.

Dr. William Yaney, the eminent psychiatrist of Beverly Hills, California, who with the help of a good trance medium includes reincarnation therapy in his treatment of patients, told one male patient that the terrible pains in his legs were due to his having lost his legs in another lifetime. The patient accepted the explanation and learned to live with his problem. But unless the medium gives specific data, such as names, dates, and places, the past-life material—even when it turns out to be beneficial to the patient—is rarely more than just another psychological trick.

Past lives are sometimes blamed for actions in this life that would otherwise be socially unacceptable. A publisher of esoteric books and audiotapes divorced his wife after meeting a young woman whom he fancied immediately. His rationalization? They had been together in another lifetime and needed to resume their partnership in this one.

What, then, is one to do to avoid being taken in by one of these past-lives readers, who, incidentally, may fully believe in their work and its authenticity? There aren't that many conscious frauds among them, but there are quite a few self-deluded persons (even they may help a client on occasion, though not in the way they think). If you are on an honest quest for truth, you must take certain precautions when dealing with past-lives readers.

First, never volunteer information about yourself or about

who you think you were in a prior life. Don't answer any questions by the reader along these lines either. Second, if the reader tells you of an existence in another life, insist on details: when, where, what name. Chances are, the reader will do one of two things: make up details that sound substantial or tell you, "Sorry, I don't get those details." Either way, take everything you are told with a big grain of salt.

True, acceptable past-life evidence is, of course, always possible. But in all the years of my practice in parapsychology, I have found that a person almost never deliberately searches out evidence of a past life. Instead, signs suggesting that regressive hypnosis might have positive results must be present before a search is undertaken, and it should be done by a professionally trained person, not a housewife or a salesperson turned past-life reader by her or his own volition.

Signs that would favor a search include recurrent dreams, where identical dreams keep coming back and are well recalled on awakening; extended déjà vu experiences in a place in which the percipient has not been before; and finally, knowledge or ability that has not been consciously acquired in this lifetime, such as the ability to understand an unknown language, the possession of technical knowledge, or "memories" of places and situations with which one is not familiar in normal life and about which one has had no access to knowledge (through books, newspapers, television, or other sources).

If you observe these signposts carefully, pursuing the quest for evidence of past lives can be stimulating and truly worthwhile. We all have lived before, but most of us have no conscious knowledge of having done so. My own records show that those who do, or who are able to recall past lives under regression, are nearly always people whose previous lives came to abrupt or violent ends.

Pat Craig

Joseph DeLouise

Theresa Dratler

Judy Hoffman

Elizabeth Joyce

Kathleen Karter

Pat Morton

Rosanna Rogers

Marisa Serbinov

Johanna Sherman

Yolana, America's top psychic

Great Psychics of the Past

Betty Ritter

Sybil Leek

Ethel Johnson Myers (with Hans Holzer)

Carolyn Chapman

Great American Mediums
of the Past

So you think that ghosts are usually found in British castles, rattling chains and bemoaning their sad fates? That the best mediums live in England? Both assumptions would be erroneous. Ghosts have been found everywhere in the world, from past times to the very present, and some of the best mediums have lived and worked in the United States. I know, because I was privileged to work with them in my investigations.

Often called the dean of mediums, Carolyn Chapman, a true Southern lady from the Carolinas, was for many years the oldest practicing medium and clairvoyant in New York. For a long time she saw her clients at a tidy and very artistic apartment in the Ansonia, a landmark on Broadway at Seventy-third Street. Later, she moved to a modern flat on East Thirty-fourth Street, where she worked until passing away at a very old age.

Carolyn was essentially an old-fashioned reader who worked exclusively with private clients. Many of the predictions she made to me over the years came to pass. But it was the unexpected visit of Dr. Andrew von Salza, a rejuvenation specialist from Los Angeles who had come along with a client, that threw Carolyn for a loop, so to speak. The doctor routinely took Carolyn's photograph with a Polaroid camera because he thought that she was an interesting-looking woman. Picture his surprise and hers when the photograph that he had taken at her flat revealed a gentleman standing next to the medium.

"Oh how nice." Carolyn exclaimed matter-of-factly, though very surprised. "That's my late husband paying me a visit."

Carolyn had no use for generalities. When I first met her in 1960, she told me that my mother, Martha, was present and that it was her anniversary. In fact, the sitting was on November 3, the day before my late mother's birthday. Carolyn then went on to give me greetings "from John who went out rather suddenly and didn't tell the truth." Well, John LaTouche, my dear friend, died of a sudden heart attack, and only after his passing did it become known that someone else had owned his house and certain rights.

Ethel Johnson Meyers, who died just recently in her nineties, was a longtime friend and a collaborator of mine in many cases. Originally an opera singer in her native San Francisco, and later a vaudeville performer with her first husband, Albert, who was also an artist, Ethel eventually moved to New York City and became a much-sought-after vocal coach. It was not until she contemplated suicide following her husband's death and his unexpected intervention from the spirit world that Ethel became interested in psychic matters. Eventually, she added mediumship to her work, and gradually it became her main occupation. She saw clients individually, and she had weekly "development" circles at her studio on the ground floor of the Sherman Square apartment on West Seventy-third Street, a large room dominated by a grand piano and an array of intertwining plants. Never willing to limit herself to deep-trance mediumship, which she was very good at, or to clairvoyant readings, which she did for her clients, Ethel "sat" for direct-voice phenomena with her circle and eventually achieved that phase of mediumship as well. A real trooper, she sometimes accompanied me in the dead of night in quest of hauntings, getting into deep trance quickly and regardless of circumstances and always delivering the spiritual goods. There are very few like Ethel because true deep-trance mediums are indeed rare.

Once I took Ethel on a case involving a murder, a case that the police had not been able to solve. We deliberately took a detour so that she would not know the location of the house that we were going to. The moment we stopped the car, Ethel said, "What's the pianist doing here?" What pianist, I wanted to know. "Rubinstein!"

Well, the case that we were about to work on was the murder of the financier Serge Rubinstein. But to voice teacher cum medium, the name Rubinstein had to be the pianist of course.

Probably the longest investigation that I have ever conducted in a haunting involved a house on Fifth Avenue in New York City. In deep trance, Ethel brought through a gentleman who thought the year was 1873. I queried him about the landlord at the time, and he informed me rather briskly that he had a landlady and that her name was Elsie something. But, oh, he did not pay her the rent; no, he paid it to her handyman, and the handyman's name was Pat Donavan. After the investigation was over, I visited the New York Public Library. In the city directory for 1873, we found that the house in question belonged to one Isabella Clark, domiciled at 35 Perry Street. In the directory for the previous year, one Pat Donavan, laborer, was also listed at 35 Perry Street. *Elsie*, of course, is a short form of Elizabeth or Isabella.

Sybil Leek, who was originally trained as a journalist and worked for years as a documentary producer in her native England, is perhaps better known for her often-publicized involvement with "the old religion" Wicca, or witchcraft, which was her faith, not her profession. Her unusual psychic powers soon led her to seek out my assistance, and we worked and traveled together many times, both in the United States and in Europe. Sybil was also a gifted author, with many books to her credit. She eventually moved to Florida, where she died.

Once Sybil accompanied Regis Philbin and me to California's most haunted house, the Whaley House in San Diego. There she identified one of the resident ghosts as one Ann Lannay. Sure enough, as I later discovered, Anna Lannay was the maiden name of Thomas Whaley's wife. In another case, the still-officially unsolved murder of a prominent actress in 1958, Leek correctly identified the full name of the young man who had been dating the actress, and who to this day remains a suspect in the case, though he has an alibi given to him by a friend. The man has never been arrested and charged. How was Leek, but newly arrived from England, to know such things?

Betty Ritter, an Italian-American from Pennsylvania, had a great gift in clairvoyance and psychometry. I met Betty many years ago at a "blind" assembly in New York, where she and Ethel Meyers were to be introduced to an interested professional audience of investigators and researchers.

That evening Betty picked me out of the audience and informed me that an uncle of mine wished to be acknowledged. I demanded details, and immediately she said, "Well, his name is Otto, he was into music, and he had a blond wife named Alice." I was flabbergasted, of course. My uncle Otto Stransky had been a famous composer; his wife's name was indeed Alice.

Carolyn Chapman, Ethel Johnson Meyers, Sybil Leek, and Betty Ritter are over there now, on the other side, where they must be regarded as very special people, which indeed they were and are.

One further observation, based on many years of exploring the field of parapsychology: the reason why some psychic readers get only part of the future but not all or get it at a different time from the time the sitter would like is, I think, that a higher power wants us to know only that which is good for us to know at any given time in our lives—no more and no less. That, I believe, is as it should be.

6

Are You Psychic?

Michael was driving his car through the night along a lonely country road that he had never been on before. There was almost no traffic at that hour of the night. His mind kept wandering off to the performance he was to give the next day in a club far away from his home base. Suddenly, he saw another car, headlights blazing, coming toward him on the narrow road.

Michael looked again. There was no car. It was all in his head, he thought, as he resumed driving at full speed. But an inner voice kept saying, "Slow down. Slow down." He did, and a moment later another car was coming toward him, lights blazing—this time for real. Because he had slowed down, Michael was able to avoid hitting the other car, and they passed each other, just barely. The incident shook him up, of course, but it hardly surprised him, because Michael had known for a long time that he had the gift—he was psychic.

June was hoping that her application for that new, better job would lead to her getting an offer of employment. They said they would call to let her know on Wednesday. Wednesday came, and June nervously waited for the telephone to ring. The hours passed. Eventually, she would have to go out and run errands. She could not very well call her potential future employers to ask, Do I get the job? She had to wait for them to call her. When noon passed, and then two o'clock, June knew that she could wait no longer; she had to get to the market. She shrugged and went to the door. At that moment, a nagging hunch forced her to take her coat off again and sit down. Not more than a minute had passed when the telephone rang. Yes, she had gotten the job. What had made her delay her departure? June realized long before this incident that she, too, was psychic.

What, exactly, is psychic? If you receive information about future events or events that are presently occurring a distance away, and if that information proves to be accurate and to have been totally unknown to you before you receive it, the explanation is usually referred to as extrasensory perception, or the psychic sense. Parapsychologists have established that ESP is not a supernatural faculty or one to be feared: it is an integral part of the human personality, albeit one that most of us have either ignored or neglected. In primitive cultures, people have always used ESP; but as civilization tended to blur deeper natural instincts and as the environment became more crowded with distractions, that natural ability to pierce the veil of distance and time began to fade for most of us—but not for everybody.

Certain individuals possess a higher degree of ESP than others do, just as some musicians possess greater talents. The development of the psychic gift is enhanced by the ability to become very relaxed at times, to allow one's inner voice to be heard, and to follow its counsel. Those who are able to accept the psychic gift as something perfectly natural, and helpful, are also likely to make use of the gift.

The odd thing is that psychic ability works sometimes through dreams, since the conscious mind is inactive when we are asleep. But there are dreams, and then there are *dreams*: some are merely expressions of unfulfilled desires or of anxiety; some are simply the result of too large a dinner. Dreams that seem to foretell the future, prophetic dreams, are of another kind. To begin with, they seem to be far clearer than ordinary dreams, which often have confusing symbols or scenes that make no sense at all. Also, while ordinary dreams are quickly forgotten on awakening, the true psychic dream stays with a person for hours, if not days. The psychic dream contains a message about one's future, or it may be a warning, but it is usually very clear and concise.

Joe dreamed that his elder brother, Carl, whom he had not seen in over twelve years and with whom he had lost contact, would suddenly pop up again. Sure enough, two weeks after the dream, Carl appeared, big as life. He had remarried and wanted Joe to meet his new wife after their long estrangement.

Not all psychic experiences deal with danger, future events, or events occurring a distance away. Being psychic entails several kinds of true experiences.

There is the déjà vu experience, or the feeling that one is experiencing something that one has already experienced in the past. Déjà vu involves the strong feeling that one has been in a place before (though one hasn't) or has met a person before (though one is quite sure that one hasn't).

Frances had never left her native Georgia until her husband took her on their honeymoon trip to Florence, Italy. Then she suddenly felt a compulsion to run ahead of her husband to an ancient palazzo, excitedly pointing out the gate and saying that she had once lived in the palazzo. The American GI entering a certain farmhouse in Belgium during World War II told his buddies exactly what they would find at the top of the stairs—and they did, even though the GI had never been there before. The Los Angeles housewife who went to the Bavarian Inn at La Jolla, California, with her family for the first time couldn't take her eyes off the owner, and he couldn't take his off her. They got to speaking, and they knew that they had met before. But he had just arrived from Germany, and she had never been to the inn before in her life—this life, that is.

Déjà vu often indicates memories from past lives—a subject currently being studied by leading parapsychologists. The evidence, consisting of detailed knowledge of previous lives that

could not have been known to the person, is often compelling—though a vague feeling of having lived in Egypt or
Tibet is hardly enough proof.

Everybody is psychic to a degree. A hunch, intuition, a
"funny" feeling about something or someone, are all mild manifestations of psychic ability. On the other end of the scale is
deep trance, the ability to go into a state of dissociation of personality, in which a personality that is seemingly different from
one's own speaks through and from one. These manifestations
are comparatively rare. Only a trained researcher can evaluate them properly—for example, determining whether a phenomenon is a truly psychic one or is an indication of emotional
or mental disturbance. The proof will always be found in the
nature of the information and in the style of the communication coming through the entranced person.

The psychic gift manifests itself in various ways. The com-
monest are foreknowledge of events in the future or at a distance; psychometry, or the ability to touch an object and give
detailed information about its owner; and impressions obtained
when in the dream state.

Some people with psychic gifts also hear voices of the dead,
or of the living who are at a distance, especially when the dead
or the distant living have an urgent need to communicate
because of crisis conditions. Others have seen apparitions,
again of the dead and sometimes of persons living at a distance. These projections, images, occur for the purpose of contacting the psychic person and in no way represent danger. In
some religions, psychic phenomena, and the ability to perceive
them, are considered undesirable, conjuring up devils and
demons; but the truth is, nothing is more natural and more
human than the psychic ability and its proper use.

Are you psychic? Have you had true experiences of the kind
I have mentioned, or do you know anyone who has? Then you
realize that psychic abilities are merely among the many won-
drous facets of the human personality. Fear is caused by the

absence of information; since you know what psychic ability is, and how it works, you need never fear it.

So you just *knew* that it was Aunt Minnie calling before you picked up the telephone? Or what was in that letter with the foreign stamp on it before you opened and read it? No, you're not weird. You're not a witch. You've got a little ESP—extrasensory perception—like millions of people all over the world.

It's like this: some people can play the piano better than others; some have better eyes than others; and some have a finer nervous system, a more developed intuition than others. It's not supernatural; it's natural, and even desirable. Think how useful it might be to know what's up ahead.

ESP doesn't happen all the time, and you can't turn it on at will. That's the rub: you never know when it will happen. Just the same, enjoy it. It will probably help you in many ways, large and small, because all it is really is a more acute intuition. In extreme cases, that sixth sense has saved people's lives by warning them not to take a certain airplane or to avoid a certain dangerous street at night. How can that be? It's a little like radar—looking ahead and telling your mind what to watch out for. Of course, whether you heed the warning is up to you, but most people do and are glad for it.

Not every instance of ESP is pleasant: Mrs. J. B. couldn't sleep all night because she knew something was wrong with her son. Sure enough, the next morning there was that call that he had suffered an accident. Ben R. was unusually emotional when he said a casual good-bye to Louis, his old friend from college days. In his heart of hearts he knew that he would never see his friend again. A week later, Louis died.

Some people get their "messages" in dreams. When the dream is precise and clear, it is probably a psychic dream that is meant to warn you of some impending event. Dotty K. dreamed that her brand-new car had been stolen, and she even saw the street corner where it had happened. But she thought it was just her worries about the car, which had cost a lot more money than she could afford. The next morning she went to work in it, and as chance would have it, she had to park it in the street during an errand. Suddenly, she recognized the spot: it was the corner that she had seen in her dream the night before. This time she did not ignore the matter but moved her car to a nearby garage. Would the car have been stolen? Probably, but Dotty didn't want to find out.

How can you find out whether you have a psychic gift? Not everybody has experiences like knowing who is calling before the telephone is picked up or what is in a letter before it is opened. Still, you may have the gift and not realize it. Why not test yourself to find out?

One simple way to find out whether you have ESP is to get a group of people together, maybe some friends but also some persons about whom you know nothing, like friends of friends. Ask each to hand you an object that he or she carries on his or her person such as a key ring, a piece of jewelry (provided that the person has been the only one to wear it), or a watch. Take the item into your hand, relax, and say the first things that come to your mind—names of people or places, images, situations—whatever you feel like saying spontaneously. This is called psychometry, obtaining information from an object that a person has touched, and it is the simplest way to test for extrasensory perception.

Ask the people in the group not to say anything until you have finished and not to volunteer information about themselves. When you have finished "reading" an object, ask the owner how accurate you have been. If you do have some psychic ability, about one-half of your statements will be correct, although you may do better—or much worse, if you don't have any ESP ability at all.

You can ask one of the others also to try his or her hand at it, but then be sure to put the objects into envelopes and mix them up so that the person doesn't know whom he or she is reading.

How do you develop your ESP ability? The more you use it, the better it gets. Keep score of your successes and failures. Nothing is perfect, even with this extra gift. To some degree, millions of Americans have ESP and don't even realize it. In our world of computers and technology, people have little room for such things as psychic intuition; but in many lands, people take the gift for granted and don't make a fuss over predictions, dream warnings, and such.

Dreams, "the gateway to the unconscious," as I have called them, are, of course, very subjective and personal. But since at times, dreams are also universally considered portents of things to come, it is important to understand what dreaming is all about.

We all dream every night, though often we do not remember our dreams. There are actually four types of dreams: anxiety or stress dreams, dreams that include falling, nightmares, and psychic dreams.

In anxiety dreams, we find ourselves in a state of fear or upset, which usually means that something we have not fully resolved in our waking life keeps bothering us during our sleep, when the conscious mind is not operating and the unconscious mind, the free and sometimes unrestrained part of our personality, has the power to impress us. Anxiety dreams are a natural and normal part of our daily lives and do not necessarily indicate illness or the need to spend long hours and much money on psychoanalysis. More often as not, psychoanalysis does not really help resolve the underlying problems: solving them in the real world, or adjusting to them, does. A typical anxiety dream might be like one of these: You are on a train or bus or airplane, or you are trying to catch one and are very worried about missing it. You are already on board, but your luggage is not; or the luggage is inside, and you are still outside worried about losing it. Such dreams occur to many people from time to time. They do not mean that you are about to travel somewhere. Instead, the "train" (or bus or plane) represents your ongoing life, your progress into the future. The fear of not getting on the train or of losing your luggage simply means that you are concerned about your future security—whether on the job or in your personal life.

In another dream, you may find yourself back in school or in your youth, at a time when you did not yet have full responsibility for yourself. Fear of not doing well in school might indicate a basic insecurity about your work performance today; dreaming of a time when all was serene in your life and your parents took care of your needs might represent a deep desire to avoid facing up to present difficulties—sort of a dream escape into a simpler yesterday. A dream in which your boss visits your house unexpectedly and you are thrilled by it yet also embarrassed about his finding you unprepared might best be interpreted as your desire to advance on the job, to ask for a raise perhaps, and your uncertainty about whether you deserve a promotion or should ask for a raise.

Dreams in which you fall from heights, sometimes with a sense of dizziness and usually followed by a state of tiredness on awakening, are really out-of-body experiences, which are not true dreams at all. Falling dreams occur when the "traveler" returns from a faster-moving dimension (the astral) and gets back into his or her physical body, which moves at a slower speed. People have done astral travel for thousands of years, sometimes reporting events or people at a distance that they think they dreamed about; in fact their spirit bodies actually saw those events or people, and they have remembered them on awakening. Astral projections, or out-of-body experiences, are common and not in the least harmful. The dreamer may be a little tired on awakening, but after all, all travel is tiring.

Another kind of dream, better called a nightmare, is often caused by physical discomfort or illness. A nightmare can be triggered by anything from a cold or a fever to indigestion or being too hot or too cold in bed. It can be caused by having witnessed a horror movie or a real accident—anything in real life that would have been frightening, and usually that took place not long before sleeping.

Obviously, if you are dreaming of being devoured by monsters or of suffering some other kind of violence—being in a shipwreck, or drowning in the ocean, being pursued by anything from murderous people to demons and devils with horns—you are having a classical nightmare. Frequently, at the same time you will feel a kind of pressure on your chest. The very word *nightmare* derives from the old superstition that such dreams were caused by an invisible horse sitting on the person's chest.

Nightmares don't actually represent anything permanent or dangerous and should not be taken seriously as anything other than what they are. If you search your memories of what you experienced the day before, you will probably find an explanation for what caused your unconscious mind to react so violently. Your unconscious is pure emotion and cannot reason things out, so the monsters in your nightmare are real only on a purely emotional level.

In dreams of the fourth category, you experience something of a psychic nature. Psychic dreams—which are always remembered and, unlike other dreams, are often retained for a long period of time—can be warnings or prophecies. If the dream is a warning, you have a premonition or a projection of danger ahead, which can be avoided. If your dream is a prophecy, you foresee future events clearly.

When you do have a psychic dream, you should always note whether you are an outside observer of the events or take part in the action. If you are on the outside, chances are that the dream is a warning, and the events are not final. If you are a participant in the action, however, you had better take heed and be careful!

There is also the relatively rare psychic dream of a past life: such a dream will have very specific details relating to place, time, and names and will become recurrent, with little change in the scenario. Such an experience can be followed up through hypnotic regression, as I have done in valid cases, with frequent success, to get further information that could actually be verified in research sources.

We all dream, and we all have the ability to interpret what comes up when we dream. By learning to distinguish between various types of dreams, we can not only understand ourselves better but also profit from possible warnings or glimpses into the future.

7

How to Become Your Own Psychic

Undeniably, our educational system does not allow much room for learning about the occult, mysticism, or any form of the irrational. European schools do not necessarily include such subjects or sanction their study either, but the cultural environment is less judgmental about exploration of these areas as a matter of course. Here, foreign-born or first-generation Americans, Native Americans, and African-Americans have less prejudice against the possibility of an occult world than the rest of the population does. Regardless of cultural prejudices, there does not seem to be any particular preponderance of national backgrounds among psychics. Nearly all nationalities and religious backgrounds are represented among those I have personally investigated.

When private individuals practice some form of occultism, there is always a potential conflict with the individual's religious persuasion, if that individual is an orthodox practitioner. Many who have had psychic experiences, or who seek them, find themselves in a quandary if they are strict Roman Catholics or orthodox Protestants or Jews. In some cases, they suppress or ignore their psychic interests out of fear that they might endanger their souls. In other cases, they will ask for advice on whether or not they are hurting their spiritual development by engaging in psychic work. Naturally, being psychic or following a course of studies in the field in no way endangers a person's spiritual standing; if anything, it contributes to it.

Ultimately, scientific methods of parapsychology and the emotional path of religious faith will merge to provide man with a single image of the deity principle.

Despite the imposing number of psychic practitioners in this country, there are wide areas where no such individuals reside and where the services of psychic readers, mediums, Spiritualist ministers, astrologers, numerologists, and so forth, reside and thus whose services are unavailable. Some people can travel to the large cities where most psychics are located; many others cannot. Sometimes a particular practitioner of the occult acquires a great reputation, resulting in far more people wanting to consult with him or her than with lesser-known practitioners. This can be very frustrating to the potential client, since the waiting lines are very long at times.

Under these circumstances, people in rural areas who are interested in "readings" frequently form their own private circle, with one of their number serving as the amateur medium. Often, two friends start out working a Ouija board in order to learn things about the future. Others stick to the time-honored tea leaves, coffee grounds, or tarot cards.

If you live in an area in which you do not have access to professional psychics or other occult practitioners and you desire to avail yourself of such services, you might want to consider joining similarly minded persons and forming a home circle. Three or more people are sufficient, and it is important that meetings be held on the same day each week to establish a rhythmical continuity. Once the rhythm is broken, whatever psychic powers have been accumulated by the meetings will be lost again, and the work must begin from square one.

The home circle should appoint one of its members as secretary to note everything that happens during the sessions. The secretary's notes should include the actual communications, if any, as well as impressions while some member of the circle is in a state of reception, or even trance, as sometimes happens. The notes should also record group members' fleeting and minor thoughts from the moment of their meeting onward. The journals of such meetings contain valuable material, and it is not unusual for bits and pieces of information thought to be insignificant at the time to be extremely significant in retrospect. In fact, the proceedings of a home circle should be reviewed by the participants once a month to see how much of the material has already become objective reality.

Naturally, home circles do not exist for the exclusive purpose of divining the future. Much time is also spent on communication with the so-called dead, when relatives, friends, or just strangers let the circle members know of their existence in another dimension; frequently tell them about themselves; and just as frequently turn into advisors for the living, predicting events and warning of impending problems. When done in the spirit of exploration and with more than a grain of salt, this kind of communication is a fine way of delving into the occult world and, especially if the communications are genuine and turn out to be evidential, can prove to be of major benefit to some member of the circle or a friend.

Care should be taken when the advice of discarnates is sought in every detail of daily life, when the dead are asked the most trivial questions by the living, and when following the communicators' advice becomes the norm in the lives of those seeking their help. If this occurs, the use of the home circle has turned into an addiction. Such a crutch is unhealthy because it deprives the living of their sacred right—and duty—of decision making. Under karmic law, opportunities and situations are thrust at us so that we may make the right decisions in handling them. If we follow the counsel of a discarnate advisor blindly, without weighing it, just because it comes to us from that source, we are depriving ourselves of a major part of our personalities. Keep in mind that some communicators, though existing in the dimension generally referred to as spiritual, are by no means superior to the rest of us in judgment or knowledge.

One should not expect yes and no answers to leading questions. Whether the means of communication is a Ouija board (of which I have written before and which I do not particularly like), the tarot cards, a crystal ball, table tipping, or just clairvoyance, the bulk of the information must come from the other side of life. Asking questions in which definite information is given as well, with the expectation of receiving a yes or no reply, is simply fooling yourself. Even if the answer turns out to be correct in the long run, the likelihood of its having been given by a discarnate entity is not very great. Remember that our own unconscious can be tapped during home circles in exactly the same way we establish communication with another dimension.

If general questions are put to the communicating discarnate entity, such as simply asking for information concerning a person or a period of time, the burden of truth lies on the communicator in the next dimension, who then must give details from his or her own knowledge. This becomes especially evidential if the answers contain elements unknown to all those in the circle. If such information subsequently turns out to be correct, the collective unconscious of the sitters can then be ruled out as a source of that information. It is also unlikely that the answers have been communicated from one sitter to another through telepathic means.

Telepathy may be an astounding process to outsiders, but it is a common occurrence in the psychic world. Telepathy between living people is frequently the source of information in home circles. While it is desirable and remarkable, in no way dose it prove spirit communication. The only material that truly can be said to emanate from individuals in other dimensions must be detailed as to names, places, and circumstances and must be totally unknown to all those present in the circle at the time the information is received. It is not always easy to establish what is known and what is unknown to the sitters. To avoid self-delusion, sitters should examine the material in the light of their earlier experiences through the years, even dating back into childhood, to determine whether or not this information could have been known to them, consciously or unconsciously. If such possibilities have been rigorously excluded, a communication obtained in the home circle can be labeled as truly derived from spiritual sources.

There is little difference in value between an amateur home circle and a professional circle for spiritual development. Naturally, if the professional medium is very strong, the development classes will also be most effective; but I have found that most home circles eventually develop one stronger member, if indeed they do not start with one, who then becomes the leading individual, the amateur medium of the circle. Whether or not the circle is successful in raising the psychic abilities of individual members depends on the period of time during which the same members of the circle meet, the regularity of the meetings, and their congeniality. Unquestionably, the psychic power in each individual is higher when the group stays together for a period of time. In addition, some element other than the purely mathematical addition of the psychic potentials of the individuals involved enters the picture, making the overall power of the group that much greater.

Some home circles like to keep a religious air about the process by starting with a prayer and ending with one. If the members of the circle are religiously oriented, this will help them relax and perhaps establish a sense of security that the prayer may keep out undesirable elements from the spiritual world. The prayer itself has no magic powers; the belief put into it creates the feelings of security. Thus, it is entirely conceivable that a pagan incantation in lieu of a Christian prayer would have exactly the same results for the sitters, if they happen to be pagans.

Popular misconceptions to the contrary, home circles for spiritual development or psychic work do not meet in darkened rooms, with black drapes covering all windows. The need to exclude daylight exists solely in attempts at materializations, when white light could be destructive to any ectoplasmic form produced with the help of the sitters. Other than for materializations, darkness is unnecessary. On the other hand, glaring electrical lights do set up disturbing magnetic vibrations that can interfere with the success of the circle. Consequently, it is best to have relaxing, somewhat subdued lighting, or just daylight. In fact, a circle may meet outdoors in the garden, if the climate allows and noise is absent. Any form of loud noise, especially that produced by electromagnetic machinery, can be destructive to the harmony of the circle as well as to the results of the process.

The room in which a home circle meets should be well ventilated, and some air should be allowed to enter at all times. Seats should be comfortable, and it may be necessary to have water handy, as dehydration accompanies most psychic attempts. There is no need for special clothing when working in a home circle, but the more comfortable and relaxed one is, the better the results tend to be. Smoking and drinking are definitely to be avoided during or immediately before a circle meeting. It isn't wise to attempt a circle immediately after a major meal. Needless to say, any form of drug taking is not only destructive to the results of a home circle, but also incompatible with any form of psychic work. All members of the home circle should show each other respect and try to maintain an air of cooperation. Bad feelings and petty jealousies are not conducive to a successful sitting.

Some people cannot locate like-minded individuals to form even the smallest home circle and yet they want to involve themselves in psychic communication or studies. Reading the literature, watching films dealing with the subject, and other indirect ways of involvement will never take the place of personal development. Fortunately, practically everybody can develop their psychic abilities to the point of being their own medium. The sole exceptions would be a mentally deficient individual; someone under medical treatment for a major disease, whether organic or nervous; or a person so deeply skeptical that he or she would block any attempt to develop psychic abilities within themselves. The average individual, however, can induce a higher degree of receptiveness through a series of very simple techniques.

The attitude has to be one of receptiveness, that is to say, willingness to accept communications from sources in the spiritual dimension, whether these communications are good or bad, not pressing for them at any given time but accepting them when and if they come. One has to convince oneself that the spiritual communications must originate with those on the other side of life; one cannot search them out deliberately or with some particular purpose in mind. It is absolutely crucial to stay open-minded, to accept beforehand anything that might come through, and not to insist on answers to specific questions. It is equally important to have a healthy balance between wishful thinking, suggestion, imagination, and that which really transpires within oneself in the way of psychic phenomena. Always seek rational explanations for information obtained and for phenomena observed before assuming that they belong in the realm of the so-called supernatural (a term I do not accept as valid, since all psychic phenomena belong well within the range of natural experiences). This is not to say that one should deliberately try to explain away a genuine phenomenon when it occurs, but one should exercise all caution when experiencing it.

Several years ago, I was standing in my kitchen making some coffee when all of a sudden I clearly heard a voice nearby calling my name. My first thought was that I had imagined it, but then the voice came again, and I knew that it was something close to me yet from a source I could not see. I decided to check whether someone in the apartment might have called

out to me. On checking, I discovered that the only other person in the apartment was my wife, who was at that moment sitting in a chair at the opposite end of the rather large apartment. Had she called out to me, I could not have heard,
especially as the door to the kitchen had been closed. Still, I
asked whether she had perhaps thought of me and had
intended to call me. I assumed that a telepathic communication could have been taking place between her and me, but
my wife had not been thinking of me or of calling me at that
time. Just the same, I dismissed the matter as of no great consequence. The following afternoon, roughly at the same time,
I was again occupied in the kitchen, and once more the voice
called out my name, no more than perhaps one yard from
where I was standing. This time I clearly recognized the personality of the caller. Only one of my acquaintances spoke my
name in just that manner. Mr. H. had passed away rather suddenly sometime before while riding on a bus. He had left his
widow in a state bordering on shock. I was quite sure it was he
who was reaching out to me for some reason. Immediately I
checked the apartment, only to find that my wife was in her
own room and the door was closed. Thereupon I telephoned
Mr. H.'s widow and found that she was indeed in a state of
deep distress. My call helped settle her nerves, and I realized
that the communication came at a time when I could play an
important part in establishing a link between the late Mr. H.
and his widow, possibly preventing her from doing harm to
herself.

Once one has established a balanced attitude toward psychic phenomena and is willing to accept them as and when
they come, it is important to establish a rhythm of exercises
and not to interrupt that rhythm in order to build up power.
The best way to do this is to set aside fifteen to twenty minutes each day, at a time when one is sure to be alone and undis-
turbed. During that period, one is to sit alone in a quiet room,
in as comfortable a position as possible, with eyes closed and

as blank-minded as possible, and displaying a hopeful, expectant attitude. At first, this will merely be a rest period. Gradually, however, impressions will rise to the surface from the unconscious part of the mind. It is wise to keep a diary from that point onward.

These impressions may concern themselves with past events, either immediately preceding the period of meditation or further back. Some may contain elements that have escaped solution up to that time, while others may be merely symbolic in character. Eventually, matters pertaining to the so-called future will be projected on the inner screen of the mind. As one continues with these regular periods of exercise, more and more material will project itself, allowing the sitter to develop his paranormal ability in greater and greater measure. After a while, simple and short questions may be inserted into the mental computer. An answer will come up in the same manner, allowing for a certain give-and-take in the process. The queries should strictly concern oneself, a condition or problem, and leave the manner in which the answer is formulated entirely up to the source supplying it, whether that be one's own unconscious or a discarnate source.

After several weeks, or perhaps months, the individual seeker is ready to test his psychic abilities on others. With most people, psychometry (touching an object belonging to another person and deriving information about that person from it) is probably the easiest undertaking. Test yourself by requesting objects belonging to strangers. Then verify how accurate your reading has been. It is less desirable to read friends or relatives, since there is usually conscious knowledge of such persons present that would make a proper evaluation of the results more difficult. Depending upon further development, the seeker might experiment with so-called haunted houses, trying to sense a past tragedy in such places and then checking his feelings or findings afterward with people who might have knowledge of the location involved. At this stage, dream material should also be carefully monitored, since psychic communications come frequently in the dream state when the unconscious is more accessible. Self-development should continue even when a certain level of accomplishment has been attained. The more the psychic powers are used, the more they will grow.

8

Parapsychology, Superstitions, and the Devil

Not everybody is an expert in matters concerning psychic phenomena. People can at times be very fearful of things they neither understand nor know well enough to judge. To dismiss or maybe even to laugh at the notion of black cats or the number 13 or walking under a ladder as being unlucky is easy. Few people take such folk notions seriously. Superstitions like these have no basis whatever in reality.

It is more difficult to evaluate what may sound very convincing to the untrained person. In a world of many religions and cults, devils and demons still play a certain role. They are blamed for bad luck by gypsy fortune-tellers or by people who need an irrational scapegoat for their failures. Here and there, glib pseudoprofessionals put the fear of the devil into gullible people in need of help, in need of counsel.

There is indeed a devil: he's cut up into millions of pieces and dwells in the hearts of those who accept his principles. But Satan is a tangible, objective reality only to those who need to believe he is, either because they have not found a better way to understand their problems or certain experiences or because they prefer the much more direct, simplistic idea of just blaming the Prince of Darkness for all their troubles.

Beware of those who preach of devils and demons, of monsters and vampires and other creatures of the night. Such beings do not exist unless you give them life in your own mind. A number of serious researchers, including me, have been able to show that discarnate entities (dead people) can reach out to the living and sometimes overpower and use them for their own ends. In thirty years of academic work in this field, though, I have never come across a shred of evidence that a supernatural, all-powerful devil has anything whatever to do with psychic phenomena of any kind.

The idea of placing blame on demonic intervention is neither new nor unique. In some few cases, criminals who have murdered for either gains or thrills find devilish possession a great excuse. Perhaps they hope that blaming their behavior on demonic influence might confound the jury when it passes sentence on them. Entire books have been written about alleged satanic plots and more complicated networks of satanic murderers. Recently, a very grisly murder in the South was immediately attributed by local police to satanists, even though no paraphernalia, tools, or other tangible evidence of satanic worship was found. Like these police officers, many people are quick to point toward Satanism in cases of gruesome or inexplicable crimes, but they are rarely capable of judging such esoteric material, if it ever shows up, to begin with.

A good deal of Bible thumping goes on in this country, discouraging people from showing an interest in psychic experiences, astrology, ESP, and dream interpretation by labelling them devil worshippers and preaching that they should be avoided. Heavy metal music is often accused of contributing to satanic influences, but all it does is produce a lot of noise and some vile lyrics. The kind of people who will shut down a museum exhibit because they consider it obscene will also try to persecute anyone who disagrees with their view of the world and their religion. If anything is indeed satanic at all, it is this ominous threat to our freedom of expression.

The same people who are quick to label as satanic anything with which they disagree have perpetuated the idea of demonic possession. The word *demon* is Greek for spirit, but belief in demons as the coworkers of the devil developed from the thirteenth century in Christian theology. At that time, the idea of the devil as the supposed counter player to Christ was first popularized as a result of the widespread survival and popularity of ancient pagan beliefs and rites among the country folk. Just as Christ was assisted by helpful angels, so was the devil thought to be assisted by troublesome demons who might go so far as to possess a living soul to serve the devil's purposes. The church would then send a priest trained in exorcism to rid the soul of the demon and restore the possessed person to proper Christian behavior.

There is no demonic possession in need of a religious exorcist—except, of course, in films—but there is a very real case to be made for actual possession of living people by discarnates—those who have died and desire to express themselves further by taking over a living person. The possessing spirits may be psychotic or evil individuals, but they are not devils or demons, nor do they have any kind of supernatural powers other than their ability to alter a living person's character and behavior. Possession is dealt with by a scientific form of exorcism working on both the invading entity and the host person who allowed it to occur.

Don't get me wrong. Ghosts, spirits, and the "dead" who live on in another world are very real, and so is communication with that world—but "demons" are not. Fortunately, the overwhelming majority of intelligent people know that demons, devils, and other spooks are fictional characters and quite harmless to them. Only when someone tries to pretend that they exist in order to frighten or influence people do they become a real problem.

9

When Is a Psychic Not a Psychic?
Questionable Practices in the Field

As with every profession, the practice of psychic work has its categories of people who are engaged in it for various reasons. Not all doctors are capable of helping their patients, and not all lawyers are competent attorneys. One should not condemn an entire profession, especially one already beleaguered by prejudice and ignorance, for the transgressions of a few.

Truly great psychics don't advertise: they don't have to. They are too busy. Many professionals who may have a real psychic gift possess an even greater gift of self-promotion that unfortunately borders on the unethical at times. There is nothing inherently illegal in self-hype, but these practices do not help the credibility of the field in the public eye. Making a decent living as a psychic is no more immoral than making a living as a doctor or a lawyer. But good doctors and lawyers don't send out hard-sell brochures via mailing lists they purchase from professional advertising and promotion agencies, either.

For the past several years, an epidemic of "telephone psychics" has hit the newspapers and tabloid weeklies, and even some otherwise respectable magazines have succumbed to the lure of easy money by accepting such advertisements. "Telephone psychics amaze callers with their powers" (at $3.49 per minute) screams one ad. "Control your destiny—readings by *live* psychics" (at $5 for the first minute, $3 thereafter—and they will keep you on the phone with double-talk and banal generalities for as long as you, poor sucker, will allow) screams another. Dozens upon dozens of ads offer readings by psychics billed as "gifted" or "psychic experts for lovers and family" or "world-renowned psychics" and so on and so forth. Even a successful singer like Dionne Warwicke has headed up a very lucrative televised network of psychic readers.

These advertised telephone readings can cost a caller very large sums of money. What's worse is that the vast majority of these so-called psychics are not in any way genuine. Now and then, a genuine psychic in need of work or cash will join one of these outfits, and the client really does get something more than generalities for his or her money. Perhaps people like Dionne Warwicke and others mean well and have a genuine interest in the psychic field. They may even be psychic themselves. Judging by the pat answers given callers by the majority of telephone gurus, however, these "psychics" must be working from instruction sheets listing certain phrases that are suitable to what the caller will usually want to hear about. 900-number psychic readings do not perform a useful service any more than 900-number prostitutes and masseuses do although, as P. T. Barnum once stated, "there is a sucker born every minute."

Equally questionable in merit is a group of guileless self-proclaimed metaphysical individuals who usually come from pretty ordinary and even dull backgrounds but somehow discover their uniqueness and wish to share it with the masses of believers. More often than not, they profess coming "from the stars" and not being really like the rest of us earthlings. These so-called specialists in cosmic consciousness may do no great harm, but they usually offer nothing more than a philosophy of their own making.

Closely related to the popularization of channeling is the proliferation of so-called past-lives readings. In the latter, a psychic will tell a client right off the bat who the client was in previous lives. Usually, the details of such earlier lifetimes cannot be checked out scientifically, as they ought to be. One should approach such readings with a healthy dose of skepticism, as there is usually little of substance to be gained from them.

All this works to the detriment of hard-working, established psychics, whose track records speak for them. Ultimately, it works to the detriment of people in need of authentic readings and, perhaps, a glimpse at some piece of the future, if possible.

10

Genuine Psychic Healing
and Healers

Sometimes the gift of the psychic, of mediumship of one kind or another, comes hand in hand with the gift of healing. Resistance by the conservative establishment toward any kind of psychic practice has often been strong, but when it comes to healing, the resistance in some quarters becomes fierce and blindly intolerant. Fortunately, the attitude of the medical establishment is softening, and the United States government has recently established an office for the investigation of alternative medicine, significantly raising the profile—and increasing the credibility—of the field of psychic healing.

In light of so many incurable diseases haunting mankind these days, from herpes to AIDS to cancer, and many more, any method of healing that works ought to be welcome. Perhaps the wisest course is to combine the best traditional medicine and alternative therapies for the benefit of the patient. Sometimes this is not possible, because the approaches and philosophies behind each doctrine are at odds with one another. But when traditional forms of medicine hold no hope, it is only ethical, I believe, to make the patient aware of his alternatives. One such alternative is psychic healing.

James Douglas DePass, of Atlanta, Georgia, an author and officer of the local chapter of the Theosophical Society, consulted Betty Dye, a psychic healer, in December 1970. Mrs. Dye, a simple housewife who had the gift, wasn't told anything about her visitor's complaints. Immediately, she went into a state of trance, during which one of her so-called spirit controls, who had been a medical doctor while in the flesh, came forth through Mrs. Dye and diagnosed DePass's ailment as stomach trouble. Speaking through the medium, but in his own voice, the doctor from beyond then placed Mrs. Dye's hands on DePass's stomach. DePass had been in continual pain (he suffered from unexplained stomach trouble and nausea), but the moment Mrs. Dye's hands were placed on his body the pains left. He walked out a well man, free from further pain in the days to come.

Mrs. Floyd Cummings came to Betty Dye in a state of abject fear: her doctor had told her she had a growth in her throat and that surgery was necessary. This is how Mrs. Cummings relates it—"The day before surgery I went to see Betty Dye, who gave me psychic healing. During the treatment I experienced a wonderful feeling of cleansing and extreme heat coming from the hands of the medium while she was in trance. When I went to the doctor afterward, the growth had completely disappeared. It has not come back since."

Betty Dye could be reached at P.O. Box 69, Union, Georgia 30291, when last contacted. She is one of perhaps a dozen psychic healers in this country who have been gaining a reputation of helping where conventional medicine can't. Unorthodox treatment should never replace ordinary medical methods, except when a patient clearly prefers them—such as with some surgery, chemical treatments, and antibiotics—because the patient believes in "natural" ways of dealing with disease. But it is the earmark of the reliable psychic healer to have a potential patient get a regular medical checkup *first*.

The basic difference between conventional medicine and the various forms of psychic healing has been summed up recently by Dr. William McGarey, a medical doctor who heads the Edgar Cayce Clinic in Phoenix, Arizona. "The way Cayce looked at it," Dr. McGarey explained to me, "an individual is first of all a spiritual being and manifests, through the mind, as a material being. The spirit creates, and the physical body is the result. But in traditional medicine, we think of structure: a man has liver disease, or lung disease. The way Cayce sees it is that one of the forces within the body has become unbalanced with the other forces."

The Cayce approach to healing is based on Edgar Cayce's revelations. This amazing man was a simple photographer in life, but when in deep trance, he was able to diagnose diseases and prescribe sometimes extremely intricate medications— knowledge he could not possibly possess in a waking condition. The Cayce readings have long become the basis of a foundation, the Association for Research and Enlightenment in Virginia Beach, Virginia, where people can get information on a larger number of ailments.

What exactly *is* psychic healing? A lot of confusion exists in the mind of the average person as to what psychic healing is and how it works. If one is to grasp the significance of Mrs. Dye's and Cayce's seemingly impossible cures, one has to accept the duality of man as the rational basis—a physical body on the outside, but a finer, etheric body or soul underneath. Psychic healing is always holistic; the entire person is healed, physical body and etheric body. One cannot treat one and not the other.

A number of healing processes differ from currently accepted medical practice. They are as old as mankind and have existed in various forms and under various names. In ancient times, such healings were considered miraculous (or sometimes diabolic). Only in recent years has an orderly, reasonable, scientific approach been possible. Today, more and more members of the medical profession are taking another look at these seemingly impossible cures, where a scant five or ten years ago, the subject could not even be discussed with them.

First, there is psychic healing proper. Here the healer draws energy from his physical body, mainly from the two solar plexus in back of the stomach and at the top of the head, where ganglia of nerves come together. This energy is then channeled through his hands and applied to the *aura*, or the magnetic field extending somewhat beyond the physical body, of the patient. A good healer notices a discolored aura. Discoloration indicates illness. By placing his energy into the troubled areas of the aura, the healer displaces the diseased particles and momentarily creates a vacuum. Into this vacuum healthy electrically charged particles rush to fill the gap in the aura. Instant healing is the result, since the physical body must fall in line with its inner etheric counterpart.

This type of psychic healer—either a man or a woman, sometimes even a youngster, for the gift plays no favorites— rarely touches the patient's skin. The healing takes place at the periphery of the aura, where it is most sensitive. Healing may take place whether the patient believes in psychic healing or not. It is a purely mechanical process, and its success depends on the healer's ability to draw enough of his life force into his hands to effect the healing. Psychic healers who are Spiritualists prefer to attribute their successes to the intervention of spirit controls, but I find that some non-Spiritualists and even some atheists have had remarkable results.

Physical healing, the second kind of unorthodox treatment, consists of the healer's touching the body in the afflicted areas. This "laying on of hands" has been practiced by many religions, and even today it is at least symbolically part of church ritual for many Christian denominations. Although the prime force in this kind of treatment is still the psychic energy of the healer, a positive attitude toward it on the part of the patient is helpful. When the healer is also a priest or minister, religious faith enters the process to some extent.

Hypnotherapy as a form of psychic healing is a method in which the patient undergoes deep hypnosis so that he or she may effect self-healing. The healer explores emotional conflicts within the patient, removes them, and replaces them with positive, helpful suggestions. By placing such low-key commands, or hypnotic suggestions, into the unconscious mind of the patient, the healer helps the patient overcome his ailments, using his own psychic energies in the process.

Faith healing is often confused with psychic healing, but the two methods have little in common. In faith healing everything depends on three elements. First, the afflicted person must have a religious belief in the power of healing (and in the intercession of divine forces); the more fervent the belief, the better. Second, the patient must have unlimited confidence in the healer from whom he expects "the miracle." Third, a large audience, the larger the better, is usually a must for the faith healing to succeed. The late Katherine Kuhlman is a prime example of the acclaimed faith healer. She never took credit for the considerable number of cures taking place right in front of the crowd, but she did hint at divine will working through her as the originator of the seeming miracle.

Successful faith healings are not necessarily the result of religious belief alone. In invoking spiritual guidance, the faith healer unleashes within himself psychic forces that are utilized to heal the sick. The expectant state in which the usually desperate patient finds himself, often to the point of hysteria, in turn spurs his own healing powers to higher performance, and so the result may be spontaneous cure. The reservoir of human psychic energy represented by the large audience is also drawn upon to supply additional power for the process.

Occasionally, however, faith healing can work without the psychic benefits of a large audience. Fourteen-year-old Cecile Diamond suffered from inflammation of the brain. Doctors gave her one chance in a hundred of survival. Rabbi Solomon Friedlander, a spiritual healer, placed an amulet in Cecile's hand and prayed. The next day the girl felt better and was able to leave the hospital soon after, completely cured.

Dr. John Myers, a London dentist who passed on in 1973, had for years tried to organize psychic healers into an association in his native England, but he never succeeded. He was, however, successful in healing R. L. Parish, an American businessman who was suffering from a chronic sciatic condition as well as from incurable near-blindness. Mr. Parish had been sent to Myers as a last resort. A few days after Myers treated him, Parish was totally without pain for the first time in years, and he was also able to discard his heavy eyeglasses.

Interestingly, Myers was even able to heal himself, something few psychic healers can do. In 1957 he suffered a serious hemorrhage and was rushed to Medical Arts Hospital in New York in the middle of the night. A panel of specialists agreed that Myers had a growth near his right kidney and that an immediate operation was in order if he was to survive. But the psychic healer refused to undergo surgery and informed his doctors that, instead, he would do for himself what he had often done for others. He remained in the hospital for one week, concentrating on his own healing. By the end of the week, the growth had disappeared, and Myers went home. The following year, he came down with an acute inflammation of the appendix, a condition which can be fatal if not immediately attended to. Again, Myers refused an operation: two hours later, all pain had ceased and an examination revealed that the inflammation had completely disappeared.

A former musician from Brooklyn seems well on his way to walking in the late John Myers's footsteps. Dean Kraft, who works with medical doctors and often goes into hospitals to minister to patients with their doctors' approval, discovered his supernormal abilities by accident, as it were, in November 1972. He was driving home from work when he heard a strange clicking sound and found the car doors locked though he had not touched the appropriate buttons. He asked aloud, more as a joke than seriously, if there were spirits present. To his amazement, he received an answer in a sort of code of clicks. At the time Kraft was employed in a music shop. Together with his boss, he perfected this code until he could actually communicate with "them."

One day Kraft heard the horrible sounds of an automobile crash outside the shop. He rushed to the street and found a woman on the pavement who had been badly hurt. Something told him to hold her in his hands until an ambulance came to take her to the hospital. Later, when he drove home, the unseen communicators told him, via the click code, "tonight your hands were used for healing." Kraft did not understand the message, but when he checked on the woman's condition, the hospital told him she was on the critical list and would undergo surgery in the morning. Placing a telephone call the next day to find out how she was doing after the surgery, he was shocked to hear she had been discharged. Somehow her injuries had healed themselves during the early hours of the morning, he was told.

Today, Kraft is so busy that it takes weeks to get an appointment with him. He doesn't advertise, and he doesn't need to. Word of mouth gets around. He freely admits that he does not always succeed with patients. But the times when he does are impressive. Half of the patients Kraft sees are referred to him by doctors. One doctor was so impressed with Kraft's ability that he helped him set up the nonprofit Foundation for Psycho-Energetic Research.

Frequently, Kraft has a physician present when he gives treatments. He starts by slightly darkening the room, then proceeds to touch the patient's head and neck gently; during this stage of the treatment, Kraft feels he is "charging up his batteries." The healing takes about five minutes, but afterward Kraft has to rest for a while—it takes a lot of energy out of him, he claims. He has had particularly good success with psoriasis, tumors, and some forms of cancer.

Kraft's powers have worked seeming miracles. One time he was called to the North Shore Community Hospital, where a patient was dying of cancer of the colon. Kraft treated the man a couple of times. The man is still alive today. Kraft has cured another man who had leukemia; he saw him two days in a row and saved him. A judge who suffered from an incurable arthritic condition in his knees and back called on Dean Kraft for help. After a few treatments, the pains left the judge and have never returned.

Dean Kraft is considered a "touch healer" who can cure people by the laying on of his hands. More often than not, the results are overwhelming and lasting. Kraft's skills were brought to the attention of President Clinton last year, but it turned out that the Deputy Director of the Office for Alternative Medicine, Dr. Daniel Eskinazi, was already aware of Kraft's work. Representative Julia Howard of the North Carolina General Assembly, the State Legislature, witnessed how her husband, suffering from incurable sclerosis, was immeasurably helped and eventually cured by Kraft's treatments. Kraft has arrested cancer through touch therapy in the case of Dorothea B. Chapman, M.D.

Kraft insists on checking up on his patients after he treats them, to make sure the cure is permanent. He also teaches his methods, claiming that others can acquire his ability, too. Dr. Michael Smith of Lincoln Hospital, Bronx, New York, has been using Kraft's methods successfully himself. So has neurologist Dr. Gabriel Rubin. Psychiatrist Dr. Abraham Weinberg of New York considers psychic healing as demonstrated by Dean Kraft "a valuable adjunct" to medical treatment.

Clearly, something happens to patients when Kraft touches them. According to Brian G.M. Durie, M.D., Professor of Medicine at UCLA and Cedars-Sinai Medical Center, a cancer specialist, Kraft's ability to transfer healing energy is worthy of further studies. Dean Kraft can be reached in Los Angeles at (310) 459-7564 or via his service number, (310) 286-1431. However, he also spends much time in his Amsterdam office, which can be contacted from America at 011-3120-627-7677.

When it comes to bioenergetic forces, Ze'ev Kolman must be one of the greatest paranormal healers of this age. By comparison, most of the other healers I have personally investigated and been treated by are much less powerful, though no less well intentioned.

In 1969 Kolman was stationed in the Sinai Desert as part of his military service, at a base called Uhom Hasiba. At 4:00 A.M. one day, restless, he decided to take a walk up a mountain near the base. There he had a close encounter with a UFO and unaccountably lost a great deal of time during which he must have been on that mountain. When he returned to the base he was a different man. He discovered that the touch of his hand caused electrical discharges to the extent that people he touched experienced the equivalent of an electric shock. Soon Kolman discovered he could heal the sick. Gradually this quiet, ordinary businessman—his family owned a dry-goods store—became Israel's most famous psychic healer. People from all walks of life have since consulted him, and many were cured of illnesses conventional medical treatment had failed to cure. Some Hollywood celebrities, major politicians from Washington and elsewhere, and a vast and increasing number of ordinary people have flocked to this man because he has indeed healed the sick in many cases, sometimes with a single treatment.

Kolman himself is not a cultist or religious fanatic. He is a man dedicated to scientific exploration of the gift he refers to as *bioenergy*, or life force. Kolman believes that his power is derived not from some extraterrestrial force (though that may have unleashed it originally) nor from spirit intervention, but from his own, somehow "activated" physical body.

"I personally experienced his therapy and was truly impressed," states Barry D. Mink, M.D., an internist practicing in Aspen, Colorado. "I experienced a great increase in physical energy, mental clarity," singer John Denver wrote to Kolman after a session. Prince Alfred von Liechtenstein, president of the Vienna International Academy for the Study of the Future, asked Kolman to treat a close friend, a lady who had suffered serious eye damage from the wearing of experimental extended-wear contact lenses and was in great pain. The lady received three treatments from Ze'ev Kolman within a span of two weeks, at the end of which she was completely cured. "I am personally familiar with Mr. Kolman's ability as a healer," stated Senator Claiborne Pell, and Dr. Enrique J. Teuscher, a practicing neurologist, wrote that Ze'ev Kolman "is a bioenergist of extraordinary ability."

Kolman has successfully treated cancerous tumors, a punctured lung, broken bones, lost hearing, and many other illnesses. Ze'ev Kolman lives in Israel but travels worldwide; he sees people in America from time to time, when he works in clinics in Los Angeles and New York. He can be reached at 50 West 34th Street, Suite 7C6, New York, New York 10001, or by telephone at (212) 564-5006.

11

Where the Psychics Are

I have no doubt whatsoever that considerable numbers of individuals are gifted by nature with the ability to foretell future events, to speak of past events or events occurring a distance away of which they could not possibly have any knowledge, and to pierce in many ways the conventional curtain of time and space as we have long known it to exist in a world ruled by rational thinking. A fair number among them are extraordinarily gifted, many are good (though not necessarily all the time and with every client), and some are bad, albeit sincere.

Only psychics who are known to me are included in this register. Undoubtedly, many gifted practitioners will be left out simply because they are as yet not known to me personally. This in no way implies that anyone who is not in this directory is necessarily without talent.

Wherever possible, I have included the address and telephone number of each psychic listed. Some practitioners, however, are not inclined to divulge their phone numbers, and I respect their wish to be contacted solely by letter. I would urge you to respect their privacy as well and to exercise courtesy whenever and however you contact a practitioner.

In addition to providing a brief background on each psychic, noting in particular any specialization or limitation of the psychic's talent, I've taken the liberty of "rating" each practitioner. The rating given each psychic is based on my own opinion of that psychic and on the reputation of the psychic in the industry. A four-star rating implies true greatness (these people are indeed a rarity); a three-star rating means that the psychic has superior talents in the field; a two-star rating indicates that the psychic is better than average.

It should be remembered that psychics are people who, like everyone else, have good days and bad days and who may have different levels of success with different people.

United States

California
Paula Deitch
Jim Downey
Irene Hird
Ruth Laker Maybrook
Maria Moreno
Maria Papapetros
Anni Pignatelli
Kevin Ryerson
Sheri Sidebotham
Damien Simpson
Ron Warmoth

Delaware
Judith Richardson
Haimes

Florida
Risa Cronin

Georgia
Pat Craig

Illinois
Frederick de Arechaga
Joseph DeLouise
Irene Hughes

Louisiana
Valerie Svolos Taylor

Maryland
Eva Marino
Daryl Jason

Michigan
Char

Missouri
Beverly Jaegers

Nevada
Cattel

New Jersey
Dorothy Allison
Joy Herald
Elizabeth Joyce
Morgan

New York
Ron Bard
Cesar Bernardo
Mary Blake
Theresa Dratler
M. B. Dykshoorn
The Enchantments
Judy Hoffman
Iana
Kathleen Karter
Leo Martello
Maria Papapetros
Catherine Paretti
Raja
Lucy Rivera
Rosanna Rogers
Marisa Serbinov
Johanna Sherman
Chuck Wagner
Yolana (Lassaw)

Ohio
Rosanna Rogers

Oklahoma
Joyce Winner

Tennessee
Pat Morton
Pat Sisson

Texas
Marion Dyone Hensley

Overseas

Australia
John Gaudry

England
Doris Collins
Richard Gardner
Ronald Hearn
Pauline Chisnall
Maddock

The Netherlands
Jan Cornelius van der
Heide

★★★ Allison, Dorothy

ADDRESS: *118 Raymond Avenue, Nutley, NJ 07110*
TELEPHONE: *Unlisted*

Dorothy Allison has received some public attention during the last few years because of her work with the police in New Jersey. When all attempts by police had failed, she located the body of a missing person, giving an exact description of the place she saw clairvoyantly. Eventually, she was able to accompany local police to the site she had envisioned. Her prediction of the victim's death and psychic vision of the body's location proved only too accurate.

Understandably, Dorothy Allison shuns the limelight. She is a very private person and does not like to give interviews. Nor does she seek clients, having come into the world of professional psychics rather by accident when she foresaw certain events regarding friends and family. She works primarily as a psychic sleuth to whom people can turn when someone is missing and foul play is suspected.

All details of her successfully solved crimes are confidential, especially as not all the criminals she has pinpointed have yet been apprehended.

She is not a "reader" in the traditional sense, dispensing counsel in all sorts of mundane matters from business to love, and she wishes to not be consulted in such matters. But when it comes to missing persons and crime matters, Dorothy Allison is the best person to consult in the eastern United States.

★★★ de Arechaga, Frederick (Ordun)

ADDRESS: *The Sabaean Religious Order, P.O. Box 8278, Chicago, IL 60614*
TELEPHONE: *(312) 248-0791*

This very knowing and cultured gentleman, a Basque nobleman by origin, came to the United States many years ago via

Cuba and settled in Chicago with his mother. By profession an artist, by avocation a researcher in the field of pagan religions and history, Frederick de Arechaga eventually became the high priest of a very colorful temple devoted to the ancient Babylonian religion known as Sabaean. The owner of an occult shop called El Saba, he is probably one of the most erudite scholars in the field of ancient cults and religions. He refers to his psychic work as the "opening of the oracle of Om."

I have known Frederick for twenty-five years, from the day he walked into my Chicago hotel room during a book tour, dressed in a long winter coat with a scarf around his neck hanging down to his heels, through interviews for my book about neo-pagan cults, and of course as a participant in many of his carefully staged, colorful pagan rituals.

He keeps his three fields of work separate; there is the temple where he and his followers practice the ancient Mesopotamian religion of Sabaean complete with music and temple dancers, even feasts, and legal marriages. His Sabaean religion also incorporates some aspects of the ancient West African religion known as Yoruba, and Frederick has assumed the Yoruba name of Ordun.

His shop, El Saba, sells occult books and supplies, and this is his primary source of income; the temple activities are not for profit.

Finally, and without fanfare or publicity, Frederick does give private sittings as a psychic. These are usually held in his shop and sometimes at the temple during daytime. How accurate is he? A Chicago woman told me he had correctly predicted her divorce when he knew nothing about her circumstances. He told me what kind of book I would be writing next at a time when I had no idea myself.

★★★　　Bard, Ron

ADDRESS:　　*Unavailable*
TELEPHONE:　*Yonkers, NY: (914) 779-0019*

Ron Bard is the psychically talented son of famed trance medium and clairvoyant Yolana Lassaw of New York. He began his career as a psychic by giving individual readings to clients and then added a cable television show to his activities where he also did brief readings, usually quite accurately, for people calling in.

I tested Bard with objects, in this case letters in neutral envelopes with only numbers on the outside. He scored well. Among his interesting predictions was a statement, spoken to me on September 3, 1985, that there would be "fire and explosions at the World Trade Center"; years later, this prediction proved all too true. Mr. Bard once told me that I would hear from a lady with whom I had not spoken since 1984, that her name was Maria, and that someone named Thomas was involved. It turned out that Maria did call me again. I later introduced her to another friend of mine named Miss Thomas, and the two became close friends. This was three years after Mr. Bard's prediction.

One of Bard's remarkable talents is his ability to look at a photograph and give a pretty accurate reading from it. And he names names, places, and circumstances—there is nothing vague about his readings. He also does automatic writing—a form of mediumship.

Bard has certainly inherited his mother's considerable psychic gift. He consults with clients either at the studio where he tapes his cable program or at the client's home. Lately, however, he has spent most of his time working in Japan, where his reputation has also grown considerably.

★★ Bernardo, Cesar

ADDRESS: *Unavailable*
TELEPHONE: *New York, NY: (212) 567-8811*

Cesar Bernardo is a Filipino psychic, now residing in New York City, with a fine reputation of having made accurate predictions in his native country for many years. He also has the ability to diagnose illness in people by reading their auras, but he is not a healer as such, leaving the treatment of the illness to medical doctors.

I met Mr. Bernardo in New York in March 1994 through a mutual friend, Prince Alfred von Liechtenstein, who had been impressed with Bernardo's powers. The Prince saw Bernardo come up with details about an Austrian inventor's work that he could not possibly have known. An amazing sidelight to this psychic's particular abilities turned out to be his ability to "read" cases from the past—situations that are suggested to him—and add new details to the stories with which he could not possibly be familiar.

For instance, in my presence and that of the Prince, Bernardo "tuned in" on the famous "Mayerling affair" of Austria and came up with obscure details not found in published books on the event, which nevertheless proved to be correct. Another example: when asked how many men were involved in the plot to murder Crown Prince Rudolph of Austria, he stated four. It turned out later that this was correct.

Bernardo is a friendly, articulate man who will see people if he feels he will be able to help them. He is a bit shy about giving readings, yet he does this professionally at least on a part-time basis. He also prefers to have potential clients referred to him by friends or other clients.

★★★   Blake, Mary

ADDRESS: *166 West 72nd Street, New York, NY 10023*
TELEPHONE: *(212) 724-4081*

Mary Blake is a spiritual development teacher who has conducted classes in mediumistic development for a number of years at her colorful Upper West Side apartment in Manhattan. People from all walks of life attend her classes at regular intervals, usually weekly, to meditate in unison and to learn certain breathing exercises and techniques that are conducive to the development of psychic ability such as visualization and semi-trance states.

★★ Cattel
ADDRESS: *4800 South Maryland Parkway,*
Las Vegas, NV 89119
TELEPHONE: *(702) 798-8448*

Cattel has lately acquired a reputation as an accurate psychic reader in Las Vegas. I have not met the lady in person, but she has given me psychic readings over the telephone that were quite accurate, considering she has never met me. For instance, she pinpointed areas of my professional activities about which she could not possibly have known.

★★★ Char
ADDRESS: *Unavailable*
TELEPHONE: *Detroit, MI: (313) 356-5360 or*
Los Angeles, CA: (310) 876-6301

Char resides in Detroit, her native city, as well as, at times, Los Angeles, California. I first met her on October 13, 1983, over coffee. At the time she barely knew who I was, but during our chat she told me of a movie that would be made called *The Amityville Curse*. That movie, which was based on my book of the same title, was indeed made in 1988.

Char is one of the relatively few psychics who "get" actual names, not just initials or descriptions of people. She has acquired something of a reputation, does television appearances frequently, and is a very personable young woman.

★★★ Collins, Doris
ADDRESS: *Unavailable*
TELEPHONE: *London, England: 948-3316*

Better known as an active healer and an organizer of seminars on healing, Doris Collins is also a fine psychic. Her life story has recently been published as a successful book, *A Woman of Spirit.*

I first met Doris at one of the many gatherings she organizes from time to time. The focus of this seminar was psychic healing. A woman of considerable talent, she has spoken at the Royal Albert Hall, with audiences in the thousands. Her healing services continue to attract large crowds.

★★ Craig, Pat

ADDRESS: *3130 Granada Way, Gainesville, GA 30506*
TELEPHONE: *(404) 532-1251*

Pat Craig, a native of North Carolina in her forties, is a mother and housewife as well as a professional psychic. A near-death experience alerted her to a world quite different from her Baptist upbringing, and an interest in psychic matters ensued.

In October 1993 she told a client who was distressed over a broken marriage that her husband would return within three days to pay her a visit and eventually would come back for good. He came back two days later and was indeed back for good by Christmas, just as Pat had predicted.

Pat has been successful in providing psychic readings over the telephone. On a whim, one client asked Pat when she might have news from a friend named Gerald. Without a moment's hesitation, Pat told the caller that she would hear from the man on the ninth of the following month, April. The caller laughed because she had not heard from him in fifteen years. Nevertheless, on the tenth of April, he did indeed call her.

★★ Cronin, Risa

ADDRESS: *Unavailable*
TELEPHONE: *Orlando, FL: (407) 265-2880*

Risa Cronin, an identical twin, worked for years in New York as one of the best typists around. She has always had a psychic gift and a love for the tarot cards. Eventually, she moved to Florida and became a professional psychic reader, developing a very good reputation in the field. Although she prefers seeing clients in person, she also does readings by telephone.

Risa uses the tarot cards for her interpretations; she names names and situations as she sees them. While most psychics have difficulty pinpointing dates of future events predicted, Risa seems to me to be very good at time, too. In two instances she has told me specifically when I could expect a response to a book proposal I had submitted to a publisher and what the outcome would be. Risa also excels at matters pertaining to romance; she told a friend of mine to forget about a certain romantic link, even though my friend did not particularly want to hear that sort of message. Ultimately, Risa's advice proved to be quite wise.

Over the years, I have found this gifted psychic quite impressive.

★★   Deitch, Paula

ADDRESS: *Unavailable*
TELEPHONE: *Sherman Oaks, CA: (818) 501-0269*

Paula Deitch has acquired a reputation as a reliable psychic in the Los Angeles area. I have never met her in person but have spoken with her several times, as well as to people who have been her clients. During one telephone conversation she predicted that I would soon be planning to come to California but that the trip would be canceled at the last moment. This is precisely what happened.

One of the younger psychics on the West Coast, Paula does not seek publicity but attracts her clients, as all true psychics do, by word of mouth.

★★★ DeLouise, Joseph

ADDRESS: *Unavailable*

TELEPHONE: *Chicago, IL: (312) 332-1841*

Joseph DeLouise was a busy Chicago barber when he discovered the gift of prophecy many years ago. During the late 1960s, he was truly a "hot" psychic who received lots of newspaper publicity, some of it self-serving but much of it honestly deserved. Sudden fame gave DeLouise a feeling of destiny and resulting power, and he set about to turn his natural gift into a professional pursuit.

Probably the best known of his predictions to come true was the surprising foretelling of a West Virginia bridge disaster, but DeLouise consistently broke into the news throughout the late 1960s because of his remarkable gift of foretelling events. In 1968 alone, for instance, he predicted financial difficulties for the McCormick Place, a Chicago exhibition hall. Months later, his prediction proved to be accurate. He also predicted that then-governor Otto Kerner of Illinois would not seek reelection and that Richard Ogilvie would succeed him, all of which happened many months later. There would be some kind of an insurrection in Chicago, he predicted on January 8; on April 7 of that year, after the assassination of Martin Luther King, Jr., huge riots broke out and five thousand federal troops were dispatched to Chicago. On a more personal level, DeLouise told a client that he saw water, and he predicted that she would have a flood in her apartment. Several days later the lady returned home to see the prediction verified. She had forgotten to turn off the water in the bathtub, and her place as well as the apartments below hers were completely flooded.

This amazing psychic is seeing people still, after almost twenty years of making predictions. The barber shop is a thing of the past.

★★ Downey, Jim

ADDRESS: *The Indigo Whollistic Health Clinic,*
554 Oakland Avenue, Oakland, CA 94611
TELEPHONE: *(800) 266-5683 or (415) 679-2320*

Jim Downey has a good reputation as a psychic and healer in northern California, where he lives. He has some college training in psychology and operates a practice in psychic counseling in Piedmont, California, across the bay from San Francisco. In addition to his psychic work, Downey is a teacher of various types of metaphysics.

In February 1980 Downey predicted before witnesses the failure of an American attempt to rescue the hostages in Iran, and he also stated that American lives would be lost. This happened in April of that year, exactly as predicted.

★★ Dratler, Theresa

ADDRESS: *Unavailable*
TELEPHONE: *New York, NY: (212) 249-6999 or*
Florida: (305) 673-6993

Theresa Dratler is an articulate, well-educated woman who specializes in tarot-card readings and astrology, but her main gift is really that of a psychic reader. Mrs. Dratler also teaches and lectures on the tarot.

While consulting her tarot deck, she dispenses advice to those seeking her out, based upon her reading of the cards as they fall. In 1987, for instance, a certain Deborah P., a registered nurse, consulted her because she felt dissatisfied with her line of work. Mrs. Dratler told her that a career in legal work would be the answer. This seemed unlikely to the client. Nevertheless, the former nurse is now a practicing attorney. In 1991 a client named Keith C. came to Mrs. Dratler because he did not like his job. The spread of the cards indicated to Mrs.

Dratler that her client should move to Florida. He did so, and he now owns three retail stores in Miami.

Mrs. Dratler came to see me on May 30, 1993, not really knowing much about me or my work. I gave her no information about myself, but she gave me a very precise appraisal of my feelings, my status, my problems—nothing specific in terms of events. Nevertheless, what she told me turned out to be quite accurate and was not likely to have been known to her.

Then, on June 21, 1993, I saw her once more. This time she predicted major events for January 1994 in my working life, and she was right. She stated that my business relations would be with a Taurus and a Scorpio. That is entirely correct.

Mrs. Dratler has a very unusual way of reading the tarot cards, unlike anyone else I have sat with. While she does not give actual names, she does describe the persons and situations she feels will occur in a client's life. With me, she did this pretty accurately and in areas of activity she could not possibly have known about.

★★★   Dykshoorn, M. B.

ADDRESS: *Unavailable*
TELEPHONE: *New York, NY: (212) 548-3448*

Mr. Dykshoorn, a Dutch-born gentleman residing in upper Manhattan, gained fame by helping the police in Holland find missing persons and reenacting murders, leading to their solution more often than not.

A true clairvoyant, Mr. Dykshoorn is about as far removed from the commercial fortune-teller as can be. He has found buried treasure three centuries after it was secreted, and he has worked seriously with the parapsychology laboratory at the University of Utrecht, in the Netherlands. His autobiography, *My Passport Says Clairvoyant*, while not exactly a bestseller, was a very interesting work describing what it is like to have that special gift.

To consult Mr. Dykshoorn on trivial matters, such as one's prospects in finance, love or such, is not advised. But those who have difficult and important cases along the lines of the above-mentioned situations will find him very businesslike and usually astonishingly accurate.

★★   Enchantments, The

ADDRESS: *341 East 9th Street, New York, NY 10003*
TELEPHONE: *(212) 228-4394*

The Enchantments is not a person but a very colorful shop in New York's East Village that sells occult supplies ranging from books to candles to jewelry, incense, and witchcraft paraphernalia of all kinds.

Among the staff are always one or two professional psychics who give readings by appointment in the back room. The people at The Enchantments are Wiccan, followers of the "white" witchcraft religion, and are very knowledgeable in matters relating to the paranormal.

★★★   Gardner, Richard

ADDRESS: *10 Sudeley Street, Brighton, England BN2 1HE*
TELEPHONE: *273-683211*

Many American travelers manage to get down to Brighton, a lovely old town filled with antique shops and interesting buildings. It is also the home of one of England's best psychics, Richard Gardner.

I have known Gardner for nearly eighteen years now and have had sessions with him that were revealing, accurate, and, I might add, very personal. Gardner, who has written several very good books, uses a deck of cards designed by an English artist, cards which in no way resemble any of the known tarot decks; also, they are far fewer in number than a deck of tarot cards.

I understand that lately Gardner has been less active due to illness, but I felt he should be included here nevertheless. A visitor to England should simply query ahead of time if a sitting would be possible. His sittings take at least an hour and deal with all aspects of one's future in great detail. Over the years he has accurately foretold my career moves and future events in my personal life—both good and bad.

★★ Gaudry, John

ADDRESS: *1212 Forsyth Street, Glebe 2037, NSW, Australia*
TELEPHONE: *660-5647*

For many years a successful actor, John Gaudry always knew he had a considerable psychic ability. Eventually he gave up acting to become a full-time professional reader, both in his native Australia and in New York City, where he spent many years in the 1970s. Having returned to Australia, where he now resides, he has acquired a large and loyal following.

Gaudry is a pleasant and honest person, and his clientele swears by his readings. He tested with me back in the seventies and did quite well, accurately predicting career matters and personal opportunities coming up.

★★★ Haimes, Judith Richardson

ADDRESS: *Frenchtown Concourse Office Bldg., Suite 6,*
             191 Christiana Road, Route 273,
             New Castle, DE 19720
TELEPHONE: *(302) 322-5439*

Judith Richardson Haimes has been a professional medium since the 1970s. She is very gifted and dedicated in a serious, no-nonsense way. Some years ago she received a good deal of publicity for having had a communication from the spirit (or alleged spirit) of John Milton, who directed her to find certain manuscripts in England.

★★★   Hearn, Ronald

ADDRESS: *Unavailable*
TELEPHONE: *London, England: 622-6857*

One of the best psychics practicing in England is Ronald Hearn, whose work I've known for many years. He is both a reader and a deep-trance medium. In the latter capacity, he worked with me on the case of the Nell Gwynn house in London's Soho, providing personal details that could only have come from the famous lady of Charles II. Americans are also familiar with his work, and he has just written a personal memoir.

While Hearn is probably the best trance medium in England today (a rare profession these days), he is also a fine reader. A session with him, which takes at least an hour, is rewarding. He has been quite accurate with me, pinpointing events that would later occur in my life as well as reading innermost feelings I rarely share with anyone. Hearn is particularly good in one-on-one sittings, of course, but can also work long-distance. He now hopes to come to America, where he already has a following.

★★★   Hensley, Marion Dyone

ADDRESS: *1609 England Road, Arlington, TX 76013*
TELEPHONE: *(817) 265-4002*

Marion Hensley, originally from Cleveland, Ohio, has been a fixture on the psychic horizon of Texas for many years. At one time she conducted her own radio program in Arlington, Texas. These days she runs seminars and lectures on various aspects of psychic work. She is also a good psychic reader.

I first heard about Marion Hensley from my old friend, astrologer Lynn Palmer, and consequently telephoned her from New York on December 4, 1980. Not all of what she then told me has yet occurred, but some certainly has. She saw "floodlights . . . movies" (I am about to do movies), that "I had a child under twelve" (my younger daughter then was seven), a "divorce" (it happened in 1986), and a "TV offer . . . esoteric mysteries" (I turned down an offer from "Unsolved Mysteries" years later).

★★   Herald, Joy

ADDRESS: *434 Caldwell Drive, Wykoff, NJ 07481*
TELEPHONE: *(201) 652-1177*

Over the years, Joy Herald has gained a solid reputation as a good psychic reader and as a lecturer on the subject. She does not use cards or any other tools for her predictions or contacts, relying instead on her natural psychic gifts.

Joy Herald is not much for world predictions and publicity-seeking headlines—she is a private person. From time to time she comes to Manhattan and sees clients on the Upper West Side in a friend's apartment. She also does groups of people and on occasion has tried to handle a restless ghost (though I have advised her against doing so). As to personal matters (fortunes, if you prefer), she is quite good.

★★   Hird, Irene

ADDRESS: *39-33 Deer Run Road, Palmdale, CA 93550*
TELEPHONE: *(805) 947-2794*

This English lady now is semiretired and living in California. She is an ordained Spiritualist minister. Some of her clients have told me she has been very accurate for them.

Irene Hird has read for me several times through the years, both in person and on the telephone. On August 10, 1982, she wrote to me of an upcoming big change in my business (though she did not give me any dates) and indicated that I would meet "someone named Terry or Jerry." Ten years later, both men became important business contacts for me. Also in 1982, she

mentioned a David and a Tony; both people are very important now in my career—in 1994.

★★★ Hoffman, Judy

ADDRESS: *334 East 93rd Street, New York, NY 10128*
TELEPHONE: *(212) 534-6279*

Judy Hoffman is a personable young lady from Pittsburgh,
Pennsylvania, where she studied at Carnegie-Mellon University
and received a bachelor's degree in theater and another in writing. Having always had an interest in the paranormal, she eventually tried her hand at being a tarot reader in 1984. She had
such success that even she was surprised.

She uses ordinary playing cards, not the customary tarot
cards, in layouts of three times seven cards, one each for the
past, short-term future, and long-term future. I had heard
about Judy through my good friend, actress Tina Louise, for
whom she had read with great accuracy. I also learned that
Judy had told a Florida hotel executive the exact date when
the executive's divorce would occur, who her next husband
would be, and the exact date of his proposal of marriage—all
of which came to be. In another case, Judy told a college girl
living in New Jersey that she would meet a man named Mike
during some sort of exercise activity and that he would wear
a uniform. Sometime later the girl did meet a fellow named
Mike, a marine, while she was swimming.

Among the many things Judy told me on June 11, 1993,
was that I would be involved in "a dispute over work or money
with a woman initialed S." In January 1994 I settled a dispute
over work done by my son-in-law, and I obtained his money
from a woman with the initial S. Judy also informed me that I
would be offered an interview by CNN. I was offered one in
November of that year, but it was unfortunately canceled due
to the California fires.

★★★   Hughes, Irene

ADDRESS: *500 North Michigan Avenue, Suite 1040,*
             Chicago, IL 60611
TELEPHONE: *(312) 467-1140*

Irene Hughes is the premiere psychic of the Middle West. I have known her for many years.

She accompanied me on a ghost hunt long before Brad Steiger decided to do the same with her and record his impressions in a book called *Irene Hughes on Psychic Safari*. She has also written a book of her own called *ESPecially Irene*, with the first three letters capitalized to indicate her connection with ESP. Mrs. Hughes, who was born and raised in the South and comes from a Scottish-Indian heritage, has had the gift of second sight from early childhood.

Mrs. Hughes has two careers, one as a psychic and one as an astrologer. She keeps them as separate as possible, so that clients may contact her for either or both of these services. For several years she worked primarily as a trance medium; later she concentrated her efforts more on counseling, but she says she uses spirit communication in her work. She is controlled by what she calls a spirit teacher, though she will not divulge his name. Her sittings take half an hour. Generally, she covers both personal life and business life for her clients. Sometimes she involves herself in medical projects and healing, as well. She has on a number of occasions worked with medical doctors, without ever meeting or seeing the patient for whom she gives a diagnosis. All this is done through the mail—at present she does not administer healing directly.

In 1967 someone suggested Mrs. Hughes become an astrologer. At first she rejected the notion, but eventually she changed her mind and studied under Norman Aarons. She later taught a course in astrology herself at a community college for three semesters. It helped her understand herself and others a lot better, although she tries to stick strictly to astrological concepts when interpreting the charts she draws for her clients. "However, if something is revealed to me psychically, I then say this is a psychic impression above and beyond the mathematical calculations in your chart, for I feel that being a psychic helps me to see more deeply different meanings," she explains.

Mrs. Hughes also gives readings by mail—she is probably one of the few reputable psychics who do. She is very good at psychometry, which is how she works in police cases. For instance, someone gives her an object from a murdered individual, and she tries to get an impression of the crime.

Her predictions about headline-making figures are impressive; she predicted Vice President Agnew's downfall due to legal problems, and she had Chicago talk-show host Bob Kennedy as a witness. Earlier, Mrs. Hughes had accurately predicted the assassinations of John F. Kennedy and Robert Kennedy, the outbreak of the 1967 Near East war, and the remarriage of Jacqueline Kennedy.

She does accept new clients both for her psychic work and as an astrologer. However, many of those wishing personal interviews may have to wait as long as several months until Mrs. Hughes can clear the time for them. Her office is staffed by two full-time assistants and a secretary. She also does a syndicated newspaper column and is planning to write more books about her work.

★★   Iana

ADDRESS: *Unavailable*
TELEPHONE: *New York, NY: (212) 889-9889*

This woman, who calls herself just by her first name, was actually born Iana St. Procel in Saint Petersburg, Russia, "with a veil," she says, and is a descendant of several generations of psychics. She reads in a light trance state using the tarot cards. Her psychic gift, she says, is that she can see the human aura. She read for me on June 1, 1992, and turned out to be quite

accurate in some statements, as I look at the reading more
than a year later.

★★★   Jaegers, Beverly

ADDRESS: *The U.S. PSI Squad, P.O. Box 29396,*
            St. Louis, MO 63126
TELEPHONE: *Unavailable*

I met Beverly Jaegers many years ago on a talk show in Saint
Louis, Missouri, where she still lives. In the 1970s she had
become justly renowned for her accurate psychic work with
police in crime cases and for having organized a group called
the Psychic Rescue Squad. For eleven years and over one hundred cases Mrs. Jaegers and her helpers have actively engaged
in crime fighting through ESP, and she has included both former and active police officers in her group and work. Today
she trains people in ESP development and offers correspondence courses related to her gift and work.

Mrs. Jaegers is not exactly publicity-shy, but then she does
have some remarkable evidence of her success to offer. Missing
persons and crime and detective work in general are her forte.

★★   Jason, Daryl (Thorton)

ADDRESS: *50 Chesapeake Landing, Annapolis, MD 21403*
TELEPHONE: *Unavailable*

I met Daryl Jason for the first time in 1977 and again in June
1983. During the second reading she mentioned that I would
go to Europe to meet with a well-known person and that I would
be writing a script, with development to follow. In 1988 I did
just that.

★★★   Joyce, Elizabeth

ADDRESS: *New Visions, P.O. Box 224, Allendale, NJ 07401*
TELEPHONE: *(201) 934-8986*

I have known Elizabeth Joyce for several years now and have a complete record of her predictions and prophecies. Years ago, Miss Joyce gained fame as a model and later discovered her psychic gifts, which are truly spectacular at times. Today she is a busy practitioner of the paranormal; her work ranges from simple private sessions to lectures, seminars, a radio program, and books.

On March 25, 1993, she faxed me the following note: "The earthquake this morning in Portland, Oregon, is the pre-quake to California—between San Francisco and Santa Barbara." On July 15, 1993, she made the following written statement to me: "Giordano will be the next mayor of New York City, and a woman will be governor of New Jersey." Well, Giuliani is close enough to Giordano, and the rest came true. Miss Joyce is very good at self-promotion (not necessarily a fault, of course) and has a genuine psychic gift.

★★★★ Karter, Kathleen

ADDRESS: *66 West 94th Street, New York, NY 10025*
TELEPHONE: *(212) 663-7434*

One of a handful of truly great mediums in the United States, Kathleen Karter, a cultured and very kind lady in her middle years, is both a psychic reader and a competent trance medium and Spiritualist.

I first met her in 1975 and have kept up our correspondence ever since, occasionally to test her considerable skills and in some cases as a consultant on a psychic problem, where she served as a medium. During our first meeting, on September 24, 1975, when she knew nothing about me, she stated that my marriage would be over by 1980 (it was), that I would travel to the West Coast in connection with films having to do with apparitions (I did, when I wrote and produced some of the "In Search Of" television series in 1977), and that I would develop a society or foundation (I started the New York

Committee for the Investigation of Paranormal Occurrences two years after her prediction).

On November 18, 1975, she read for me again, this time predicting that I would cross the water in connection with an old house; there would be negotiating going on for money, and books and "things" would be moving in Europe. About three weeks later I received an unexpected offer for the house I owned in Austria. I flew over immediately and sold it after considerable negotiations; books and "things" were indeed moved out of the house and left in Europe for me.

Some things she predicted did not come true, at least not yet, and some never can, because she had put time limits on them. But the fact that Kathleen Karter got many things that occurred later on in such detail is astonishing and convincing.

★★   Maddock, Pauline Chisnall

ADDRESS: *3 Affetside Drive, Lowercroft, Bory,*
BL8 2ES, Lancaster, England
TELEPHONE: *7-06849-411*

For many years, Pauline Chisnall Maddock has been active as a spiritualist and psychic reader. She has a very considerable psychic gift and has also worked as a spiritual counselor, lecturer, and psychic artist, in that she receives impressions of communicating entities and draws their likenesses on paper.

One of the most remarkable instances of this form of communication took place several years ago when Pauline was merely an amateur psychic and still worked as a telephone operator for a large company in her city. Again and again, the image of a man with piercing eyes impressed itself on her. Finally she drew the psychic image on paper. It turned out to be the late Igor Stravinsky, the famous Russian composer.

Pauline built a following by performing mass readings; eventually she became a professional.

★★   Marino, Eva

ADDRESS: *4700 Leyden Way, Eliot City, MD 21043*
TELEPHONE: *Unavailable*

Eva Marino is not a well-known reader, but I have spoken to those who have consulted her regularly and who have been very much impressed with her work.

    I have not met her in person but have spoken with her on the telephone. In my opinion, she is authentically gifted. This has been corroborated by several friends of mine in the Nashville, Tennessee, area who have sat with her.

★★   Martello, Leo

ADDRESS: *The Magical Pagan, 22 Greenwich Avenue,*
                 New York, NY 10003
TELEPHONE: *Unavailable*

Leo Louis Martello is to the (white) witchcraft movement in the United States what Ralph Nader is to consumer fraud: he is always on the lookout for discrimination and falsehoods about one of the world's oldest religions. But Martello also has a fine psychic talent, and on occasion he will give readings. He is good.

    In earlier years Martello had been primarily known as a sometimes noisy advocate for witches' rights and as a darling of the tabloid press. But later he earned a good living in business, acquired an honorary doctorate, and is today considered a very knowledgeable occultist. I cannot disclose details of his readings, as those details are considered to be privileged information.

★★★   Maybrook, Ruth Laker

ADDRESS: *Unavailable*
TELEPHONE: *(213) 821-6219*

Ruth Maybrook spent most of her working years in the business world, filling middle-level positions and working as a consultant. But her psychic gift could not be ignored, and eventually she became a professional reader.

Her readings are more proof that time is a very elusive element with nearly all psychics, with occasional exceptions where exact times are indeed predicted. Many of the events predicted by her have come true, though not as quickly as her reading leads her to believe.

On September 25, 1985, when I first sat with her, she predicted that seven years later I would be involved with Hollywood—both in television, which would come first, then films—all of which is perfectly true. She told me I would have emotional difficulties with my wife in April 1986: we were divorced in June 1986! She mentioned a Brandon and a European named Paul; I am at this writing in touch with both of these men professionally. She predicted a forum or school where I would work with other scientists in the paranormal area, and that major people would be involved—all of this is happening now.

★★★★ Moreno, Maria

ADDRESS: *2045 E. Casa Linda Drive, West Covina, CA 91791*
TELEPHONE: *(818) 919-6126*

I first heard about a "fabulous Mexican psychic" named Maria Moreno from fellow author and researcher Jess Stearn, who had tested her and found her extremely gifted. So I made an apppointment to see her in June 1981; her English was marginal, but we understood each other, and I am sure she had no idea who I was. I simply said I had heard of her through friends.

She began this first session by going into trance and letting her control speak through her. She mentioned Dino di Laurentiis. At that time, Dino had nothing to do with me or my work: that came several years later. She mentioned a Rosemary, and I met the lady only three years later; we are still very close friends. A "big politician, P., would be helpful." I met Senator Claiborne Pell several years later for the first time. Then came what I considered the most convincing part of the session. Suddenly, Maria asked me whether I could place someone named Eileen, a lady who she felt was very important in my life—someone I had worked with—and a man named John, whom I had met through Eileen, both of whom had long passed over. I immediately recognized them to be the late Eileen Garrett and the writer John La Touche—but how could Maria know this? Quickly I looked around her modest apartment, wondering if I would find some of my books where these two people were mentioned. I found none. Frankly, Maria's English at that time was such that I doubt she could have understood such books even if she had them.

I saw Maria again on June 15, 1987, a very hot afternoon in Hollywood. Actually, she expected a "Mr. Wood," as I had decided not to use my real name. It made no difference. Her control, whom she simply called "the hunchback," took over and greeted me like an old friend. I noticed that the trance control spoke excellent English, while Maria in her waking condition never could.

This second reading was even more interesting than the first. Contracts, deals, and again, Dino di Laurentiis were mentioned. By then, though I had already met the man and encountered contractual difficulties with him. A James wanted to be acknowledged from the other side, "like a preacher," Maria said. I was very close to the late Bishop James Pike, with whom I had made a film, and about whose death I had written a book.

An institute would come about (it seems that this will finally happen this year!). The rest was personal but also very specific as to names and identities of the people mentioned—but no specific time element was given, which was no surprise. I also found it remarkable that the second reading duplicated much that had been stated in the first—though there was no way she could have taken notes during our initial session.

★★   Morgan

ADDRESS: *Unavailable*
TELEPHONE: *(201) 868-0398*

This man, who bills himself as simply Morgan, seems to have a pretty impressive track record in helping police solve crimes. He has also accurately predicted earthquakes in his home state of New Jersey, something not common in that part of the country. I met him a few years ago in Manhattan, where he has a considerable following.

★★   Morton, Pat

ADDRESS: *Unavailable*
TELEPHONE: *Nashville, TN: (615) 833-7574*

This Nashville seeress of Irish, Scots, and Indian background discovered her clairvoyant abilities as people came to her for counsel over the years.

In 1989 Pat Morton predicted that a dark-skinned Middle East leader would cause problems, including what she called a Saudi War," within two weeks—precisely when Saddam Hussein invaded Kuwait. In another successful prediction, a Memphis client asked Pat whether her daughter would win a certain beauty contest. Pat assured her only that a girl wearing a peach-colored dress would be the winner. It turned out later that the dress the girl wore was indeed peach-colored, and she won the contest.

★★   Papapetros, Maria

ADDRESS: *80 Park Avenue, New York, NY 10016*
TELEPHONE: *(212) 370-0241*

For many years, Maria Papapetros has been giving readings to her faithful clients in both Los Angeles and New York City. Her reputation is very good.

I met with Maria for the first time on March 30, 1980, at her house in the Los Angeles area. At that time I was not terribly impressed with her work because much of it was of a counseling nature rather than predictions; but one health problem she correctly foretold then was in fact diagnosed eight years later.

I met her again twice after that, and the accuracy of her readings, which were mainly of a personal nature, was quite impressive.

★★   Paretti, Catherine

ADDRESS: *600 East 70th Street, New York, NY 10021*
TELEPHONE: *(212) 472-3255*

Catherine Paretti is both a psychic and a healer, the latter the result of having suffered severe illnesses that had left her paralyzed for a long time. For eight years, she lived in a wheelchair, but her determination and efforts at self-healing eventually cured her. In 1975 she almost died and had a typical near-death experience, and in 1982 she was struck down again by a nerve disorder, only to overcome all this and become a successful practicing psychic.

In 1987 I took her on for development and saw her almost every week for psychic tests. A remarkable reading was given me by Catherine in a session on June 17, 1987, when she stated there would be "a breakthrough . . . two men clasping hands with joy . . . movies . . . entry . . . very good movie and money." Well, it was not until the summer of 1988 that I met my film partner in Europe. Our first film is in fact called *The Entry*, and after it is made, sometime this year, we will know if the rest of the prediction will also come true.

★★★   Pignatelli, Anni

ADDRESS: *Unavailable*
TELEPHONE: *Los Angeles, CA: (213) 391-3900*

I met Anni Pignatelli in Los Angeles around 1979 and consulted her on and off through 1983. I found her to be an exceptionally gifted psychic who uses both the cards and her own psychic insight to give her readings.

Sometimes her predictions, which usually lack names, only make sense much later. For instance, on February 13, 1980, Anni spoke of my attending a wedding, away from Los Angeles, and she told me that the woman would be older than the man. This did occur, but many years later.

★★   Raja

ADDRESS: *Unavailable*
TELEPHONE: *New York, NY: (212) 242-2635*

Raja studied esoteric lore and practice in India and Europe. He specializes in dream interpretation and regressive hpynosis, and he also teaches his craft. I learned of his work through a local cable show on which he appeared, and I subsequently asked him to visit me in my offices.

Raja used tarot cards to get impressions about me, and I am quite sure that his knowledge of me and my work was primarily in the field of parapsychology. Thus, when he came up with unconnected areas, I was impressed.

★★   Rivera, Lucy

ADDRESS: *Unavailable*
TELEPHONE: *Brooklyn, NY: (718) 763-9762*

While her professional life still centers around the business world, Lucy Rivera has for years also done psychic readings.

She has achieved considerable success and a good following in the greater New York area.

Lucy and I met for the first time on July 15, 1984, and have gotten together sporadically ever since. During our first meeting she psychometrized (touched) several objects as a test, which is how I usually start my evaluation of a psychic. Lucy tested fairly well, but I suspected that psychometry was perhaps not her strongest gift—as I later learned, that was indeed true.

When Lucy has a strong psychic impression, she telephones me right away, especially when the impression concerns danger or matters of national interest. Due to my connections, I have always been able to forward her warnings or visions to people in authority.

Lucy visited me on December 27, 1990, very concerned about a vision she had first had the previous year. In the vision, she saw four airplanes over Manhattan, which she felt were threatening, and she connected this to the then ongoing struggle with Saddam Hussein of Iraq. But she also "saw" a bomb going off in the Wall Street area of Manhattan and smoke rising. She described the people involved as dark-skinned, wearing a kind of blue uniform like overalls, and she saw people running all over and great turmoil. She felt that the people who had caused this came from the Newark, New Jersey, area. The same basic vision reccurred to her on January 15, 1991. She then decided to tell me about it so I could warn the authorities, which I did.

When the predicted events failed to transpire during the Persian Gulf crisis, I thought no more about it, until the terrible World Trade Center bombing took place two years later. The perpetrators did indeed include some who came from New Jersey, and the overalls were work clothes worn by them when they were posing as a repair crew to gain entry to the building.

★★★★ Rogers, Rosanna

ADDRESS: *Unavailable*
TELEPHONE: *Cleveland, OH: (216) 751-1651 or*
            New York, NY: (212) 832-1887

Rosanna Rogers was born in Austria and brought up in Germany, where she attended high school at the Convent of the Sisters of St. Francis in Pirmasens and college at the Convent of San Lioba, in Freiburg. She now lives in a colorful house in one of Cleveland's quieter districts, on Svec Avenue, and has her own local cable television program. People from many parts of the world reach out to her for predictions.

Rosanna is no ordinary fortune-teller: she is very precise and firm with her predictions for her clients. A woman I know came to consult Rosanna in the summer of 1987 during a civic fair. Her husband at the time was in prison on what she knew to be a false accusation, and she had no hope of seeing him exonerated, so she had decided to sell their apartment building. But Rosanna, who had never seen the lady before in her life, told her not to sell it because her husband would be home in time for them to share a Christmas celebration. Well, Christmas came and her husband was still in jail. But then suddenly his case took an unexpected turn, and the appellate court freed the man. The couple celebrated the following Christmas together.

I have known and worked with Rosanna since the 1970s and consider her to be the most knowledgeable tarot reader in the world. She is also a gifted psychic, even without her cards. The cards, designed and hand-painted by her, draw upon mythology as symbolism and are totally unlike any other tarot deck ever designed. Rosanna has also written a handbook to explain the usage of this very special, and very accurate, card deck.

Over the years, Rosanna has sent me predictions or made them in my presence or to reputable witnesses who have testified accordingly. Here are some of the outstanding predictions Rosanna has made.

On January 10, 1990, Rosanna said: "I see a 707 airplane, approaching the Atlantic coast, crashing. I perceive digits . . . 5?" On January 26, 1990, a Columbian airliner, Flight 52, a 707, crashed near New York City.

On September 23, 1983, she predicted that "the United States and the Soviet Union will recognize the need to work together in unison as the danger comes from nations with nothing to lose, such as Iran, Iraq, and Libya." In June–July 1990 the United States and the Soviet Union became chummy as never before, and worries about Iraq and Iran became greater than ever.

"Nixon may get out of the Watergate Affair elegantly by resigning," Rosanna said on July 19, 1973. On August 7, 1973 Nixon resigned.

During the summer of 1989, Rosanna, whom I had been monitoring carefully for thirteen years, insisted that all was not well with the President and his family. She insisted there were health problems that we would hear about soon and other problems, even more worrisome, concerning the President's immediate family. Finally, on January 10, 1990, she put her concerns in writing to me. How accurate was all this? On February 15, 1990, Barbara Bush went through surgery on her lip and dealt with an eye problem; on January 29, 1990, Neil Bush, the President's son, started having serious business problems that mounted to ominous proportions, and on April 12, 1990, the President himself discovered early signs of glaucoma.

A European-born woman with horrible memories of the Hitler era, Rosanna predicted the innocence of a man accused as a concentration-camp guard and war criminal, placing her professional integrity above her deep feelings. While the world knew that a man named John Demjanjuk, deported by the United States, was being tried in Israel because he had been identified by witnesses as "Ivan the Terrible," a particularly vicious and murderous concentration-camp guard, nobody much doubted the outcome. But Demjanjuk and his lawyer insisted all along that he was not Ivan the Terrible—that he was being wrongfully accused. Was it really a case of mistaken identity?

On January 10, 1990, Rosanna stated to me that "the Demjanjuk case will get a new twist—they've got the wrong man." Personally, I doubted it, but events proved me wrong and the Cleveland psychic right. On February 26, 1990, Polish villagers who lived near the former Treblinka concentration camp told reporters for the television program "Sixty Minutes" that the man dubbed Ivan the Terrible was really named Marchenko, not Demjanjuk. The authorities had the wrong man. On May 14, 1990, the Israeli court heard an appeal of Demjanjuk's death sentence, which had been imposed by a lower court. As a result, the Demjanjuk case was reopened and a new investigation by the court found the man innocent. He now lives quietly in Cleveland.

Moving from the very serious to the very superficial, Rosanna maintained throughout 1988 and 1989 that millionaire Donald Trump was heading for a fall. On January 10, 1990, she made this prediction: "He will learn the raw fear of losses, both emotionally and in business, but he will bounce back." On the same day, Rosanna assured me that former President Reagan would be the first president in American history to testify in court. He did, in February and March.

Rosanna lives in Cleveland, Ohio, but she visits New York City every month or so. She does consultations by telephone as well.

★★   Ryerson, Kevin

ADDRESS: *Ryerson Enterprises, P.O. Box 151080,*
            San Rafael, CA 94915
TELEPHONE: *(415) 454-9727*

Kevin Ryerson gained some prominence as one of the psychics publicized by actress Shirley MacLaine, a lady with a genuine interest in the psychic field and a somewhat uncritical approach to it.

Ryerson has become quite a successful international enterprise, lecturing, demonstrating, and traveling all over the world, giving seminars, channeling sessions, and, I assume, also individual consultations. He also does telephone readings, which many other psychics do these days.

Ryerson seems to be very good at what he does, and no doubt there are many people who enjoy his readings and lectures. He may even be as good and remarkable a psychic as he claims to be. But I really have no evidence that he is. We have attempted to induce him to test sit with us on several occasions and have gotten the cold shoulder.

★★★★ Serbinov, Marisa (Marisa Serbinov Anderson)

ADDRESS: *555 Central Park Avenue, Scarsdale, NY 10853*
TELEPHONE: *(914) 725-8871*

Marisa Serbinov is a young woman with a long career in advertising, fashion, photography, and modeling behind her. A very curious mind and an interest in the paranormal eventually led to her wanting to develop her psychic gifts.

Hers is far from the traditional image of the medium or psychic reader. Her background includes the Parsons School of Design, the Westchester Academy of Ballet, and even some work as a private investigator. She is an expert at various sports and is fluent in Russian—her father was of Cossack origin.

I met her during a lecture on parapsychology at a local college and worked with her regularly to help develop her considerable psychic gifts. I took her to some haunted locations including June Havoc's town house in Manhattan, where Marisa described "a girl waiting for a man" (Hungry Lucy and her soldier in the 18th century), and Clinton Court, where she picked up the impression of a high-ranking officer from England around 1780, and "children's games" in the 1830s (a child fell to its death on the stairs there), horses and a carriage (the house was a carriage house long ago), and, finally, someone named Harry CL—in fact, Clinton Court was originally Sir Henry Clinton's home, something she would not have known.

As a reader to private clients, Maria has had considerable success. For instance, a client named Annie D. was about to look for a used car in newspaper ads, but Marisa told her not to bother: someone she already knew would soon offer her a car. Marisa even described the car in detail. Two weeks later the woman did get such a car from the mother of a friend. Marisa warned another client, Deborah S., of a possible attack near a supermarket by a man wearing a cap, with a white van. Later, Deborah did see such a man and van at the supermarket and, having been warned, drove around him.

What is perhaps unique, or at least very rare, about Marisa's mediumship is her ability in respect to animals. She sees animal as well as human spirits who have passed over. Diagnosing the illnesses of pets seems to be part of this gift. Sally P.'s cat suddenly became ill for no apparent reason, but when Marisa touched her, she told Sally that the cat had been drugged. Sure enough, the veterinarian confirmed that the cat had swallowed some sort of pill, causing her to become ill. Marisa herself has three cats and four birds, so perhaps her environment contributes to her great empathy in dealing with animals.

★★★   Sherman, Johanna

ADDRESS: *P.O. Box 148, Brooklyn, NY 11224*
TELEPHONE: *(310) 657-5590*

For many years, Johanna Sherman was one of the busiest and best-known tarot readers in the New York area. She also became known as the creator and designer of a new tarot deck called the Sacred Rose.

These days Johanna does not seek publicity, but her clients know exactly where they can find her. Over the years I have monitored her personal readings, which frequently proved to include very accurate predictions of events that would occur years later.

If you can get a sitting with Johanna, you can expect to receive some pretty concrete information about yourself and your future. Johanna is definitely a major psychic.

★★★   Sidebotham, Sheri

ADDRESS: *Unavailable*
TELEPHONE: *(310) 657-7647 or FAX (310) 657-5590*

Sheri Sidebotham is the darling of the Hollywood set, a reliable psychic with a very large following among the elite. I met Sheri in the late seventies in Hollywood and later in New York, where she had an apartment. Her readings were highly personal and quite accurate.

Her Hollywood regulars include Joan Collins, Linda Gray, Lalo Schifrin, and many others, and she has a strong following in Latin America and Europe as well. In a sea of often questionable "psychics" that have invaded the Hollywood scene, Sheri stands out like a beacon of light. She truly possesses a straightforward psychic ability.

★★   Simpson, Damien

ADDRESS: *Unavailable*
TELEPHONE: *(310) 434-3453*

Dr. Damien Simpson just celebrated his twenty-fifth anniversary as head of the Spiritualist Universal Mind Science Church in Los Angeles, California. He is a good psychic and can be consulted individually.

★★   **Sisson, Pat**
ADDRESS: *6828 Reddeje Road, Knoxville, TN 37918*
TELEPHONE: *(615) 689-4469*

I met Pat Sisson in 1985, when she was already well known in
Tennessee as a reliable psychic reader and counselor.

  She is a true medium and has been involved in several
ghost-hunting activities. She also conducts seminars and lectures, often to business groups or clubs.

★★   **Taylor, Valerie Svolos**
ADDRESS: *951 Ontario, Shreveport, LA 71106*
TELEPHONE: *(318) 861-0930*

Valerie Taylor lives in Louisiana, but her clients live all over
the world: Europe, Asia, and the Americas.

  An acquaintance of mine, Gillian M., met Valerie in the
fall of 1992. Valerie's reading of her included pinpointing a
stomach problem, identifying the lady's husband's profession,
and predicting that the client herself would have a career in
the media. Gillian now works in national radio.

  Several years before it occurred, Valerie told another client,
Barbara D., that the United States would bomb Iraq.

  Valerie can be contacted for readings or other psychic
work.

★★★   **van der Heide, Jan Cornelius**
ADDRESS: *Schoutenburgstraat 17, 2343 XS Oegstgeest,*
                the Netherlands
TELEPHONE: *17-28-70*

A highly literate and knowledgeable man, Jan van der Heide
is both a psychic and a healer and has been involved in the
publication of magazines dealing with psychic phenomena in
his native Holland. He also works as a hypnotherapist and is
highly respected throughout Europe. In addition, while in

trance he paints portraits of spirits, a remarkable (but not unique) gift.

Jan came to my attention in 1978, and I visited him during the following year. Probably the best known of his written predictions occurred on September 13, 1978, when he stated that Pope John Paul I would be dead within four months. This was at a time when the newly elected pope seemed to be in the best of health. Of course, he died even before the four months were up—and rumors of foul play have never quite died down.

On December 29, 1990, Jan stated on radio and in writing that "there will be a short and heavy war in the Middle East. I see American bombers fly to and above Baghdad." Further, he predicted at that time that there would be a military coup in Russia and that "Gorbachev will disappear from the scene in 1991."

★★　　Wagner, Chuck

ADDRESS:　*4 Park Avenue, New York, NY 10001*
TELEPHONE:　*(212) 725-8849*

A publicity-geared tarot reader and teacher of the tarot, Chuck Wagner is nothing if not self-serving in his pursuit of fame and clients. But he is a very good reader and a nice man. He is often very accurate and very specific, and he obviously possesses considerable psychic ability.

Show-business people in particular like him, though he also works for corporations and businesses at times.

★★★　　Warmoth, Ron

ADDRESS:　*P.O. Box 4037, Los Angeles, CA 90028*
TELEPHONE:　*(213) 389-3483*

Ron Warmoth has been a practicing psychic with an excellent reputation for many years, first in the New York area, then briefly from New Orleans, and for many years now in Los

Angeles, California. His psychic abilities include dowsing (for oil and mining possibilities), business counseling, and personal readings. He also publishes a newsletter devoted to business predictions, the stock market, and other future financial trends and events.

In June 1987 a New York woman contacted Warmoth in respect to a missing person. Warmoth had to tell her that the man had been murdered, and he gave her all details as to how and why, and where the body would be found. A few weeks later, the murderer was caught. All details stated by the psychic were proven correct.

★★★ Winner, Joyce

ADDRESS: *P.O. Box 691216, Tulsa, OK 74169*
TELEPHONE: *(918) 744-9411*

Joyce Winner and I met back in 1976. She is both a psychic and a healer and has had a good reputation in both areas through the years.

In October 1977 she had the courage to tell me that my marriage "was over" (and it was) and why. She proved to be correct.

Sometimes little things mean a lot as evidence. In a reading on January 12, 1979, Joyce spoke of my writing something "about a Loch Ness monster." I did, years later. During the same reading, she told me I would travel to California, where I would meet a woman I would be close to. Joyce even mentioned the woman's unusual family name. That, too, proved accurate.

On May 22, 1980, she described a scene where she saw me with a woman named Elaine in California, at the ocean, with other people. A few years later, in 1984, I did spend an evening at a well-known actress's house on the Pacific, and my date was a friend named Elan.

In June 1982 Joyce predicted I would have some of my books reprinted. This happened in 1986.

★★★★ Yolana (Yolana Lassaw)

ADDRESS: *245 East 58th Street, New York, NY 10022*
TELEPHONE: *(212) 308-0836 or*
                      answering service: (212) 868-1121

Truly the queen of psychics, this lady can be so accurate and detailed one wonders how it is possible. Yolana often has a waiting list of would-be clients, but she gets around to most of them. Living in a place called Le Triomphe in New York, she triumphs more often than not.

Yolana Lassaw discovered her gift to "see things before they happened" when she was a housewife working a few odd jobs for a living. When I took her in hand with rigorous training, her psychic ability was new to her. Now, eighteen years later, she is usually right on target. Nobody's perfect, but if anyone among psychics is close to it, it is Yolana.

As a little girl of ten Yolana would psychically make the doorbell ring when she wanted to be let out. In 1971 she told a neighbor in Eastchester, New York, not to date a certain man because he would die of a heart attack at the wheel: he did, and the neighbor has never doubted Yolana since.

Yolana's mother read the tarot cards for friends. Yolana herself gets "impressions" about people's future even without cards. Like all psychics, Yolana can't pinpoint exact times well, so not every one of her predictions has as yet come true. But the ones that have are impressive.

On November 12, 1978, Yolana "saw" a silver and blue railroad train derail, adding that the event would take place at the end of November or in early December. On December 3, the Southern Railway Express was derailed, just as Yolana had described it.

On November 19, 1978, Yolana spoke to me of an airplane crash "over hills or mountains in suburban U.S." She told me that there would be trouble with the left wing, there would be casualties, and the figure 7 was somehow associated. The following day a light plane crashed in a suburban area on the West Coast. The left wing hit a tree coming down, and seven people were involved, six on the plane and one on the ground. Only one person survived.

On December 2, 1978, Yolana predicted the "collapse of a building in a busy part of New York City within two weeks." On December 17, a huge scaffolding on a Fifth Avenue apartment building collapsed, narrowly missing crowds.

On December 17, 1978, Yolana told me that she foresaw a bombing at a busy New York terminal right after the New Year, that people would be hurt, and that it would be the work of a crazy person, not politicals. On February 19, 1979, three teenagers set fire to a subway token booth, resulting in the deaths of three people. The motive was personal revenge.

On January 11, 1979, Yolana stated that "one oriental country would invade another very shortly." On February 17, China surprised the world by invading Vietnam.

On January 16, 1979, Yolana spoke of a "terror ride" on a train going to Coney Island. On February 26, 1979, a holdup man terrorized and victimized people on just such a train.

On November 15, 1980, Yolana confided to her secretary, Josephine Sonnenblick, a vision in which she saw someone in terrible danger near black gates: "a man gets out of a car, someone is going to be killed, it is very big—I hear many shots." Yolana thought someone named David was involved. Three days later John Lennon was shot in front of the black gates of the Dakota Apartments in New York City by a man named Mark David Chapman.

On October 15, 1985, Yolana predicted an earthquake near San Bernardino, California, that would be felt in New York. That is exactly what happened on February 18, 1986. At the same time she spoke of a "bombing by the PLO at a military base in Germany," but she was not sure about the place name, which she thought sounded like *Bogen*. Later, a nightclub frequented by American military personnel was bombed by Arab terrorists. It happened on October 24 in Berlin.

Yolana makes her living by giving readings to individuals, not by making world predictions. She has a habit of rattling off names connected with the client—often people the client meets later in life. Among twelve names she gave me on October 25, 1990, eight are of people I subsequently met and some of them have become important connections for me. Apparently, time does not exist "over there" where events are set in motion. How else could Yolana have spoken to me on May 9, 1980 (in respect to my writings), of Waldenbooks: they became my publisher twelve years later.

After a bout with illness, which forced her to work less and take greater rest periods, Yolana is now back again at full speed. On our first meeting after more than a year's separation during which she had no knowledge whatever of my ongoing life, she overwhelmed me with descriptions of situations that were just then occurring in my life and that might well result in major changes in my career and life.

On January 20, 1994, as I entered her apartment, Yolana quite spontaneously confronted me with a statement about Canada and a television and film project involving me, two people named David and Ben, and a book of mine which she identified as *Amityville*. As a matter of fact, I had just signed an agreement, via my agent Ben, with a producer named David, about a series of films based on my Amityville books. After our sitting I confirmed this to the medium, telling her that a French company was going to produce these films. She replied immediately, "Oh, no, not just a French company; several other countries are also involved." Since this was not what I had been told, I checked with David, the producer. He confirmed that several other countries were indeed also involved.

Yolana's work with the police, which she does at no charge, is truly remarkable, according to Lieutenant Riguzzi of the

Harrison, New York, homicide squad. A double murder of two young girls in 1984 was solved largely due to Yolana's leads. When she psychically receives information about a murder she falls into a semi-trance during which she states things she cannot know or recall consciously afterward. It seems certain, at least in some cases, that the deceased is giving her that information. In one case she stated, "I lost one of my cuff links." This turned out to be true: the body found was minus one cuff link. In another police case, Yolana stated that the victim "had something wrong with his ring finger"—when the body was found, it appeared the murderer could not remove a valuable ring, so he had cut off the victim's finger.

In her private practice, Yolana deals with far less gruesome matters, to be sure. Still, she sees what she sees and does not edit it or soften the blow. Detective Thomas McCue of the Greenwich, Connecticut, police confirms that Yolana, on meeting a just-married colleague of his named Bill, predicted that the marriage would last for two years and then break up. The marriage lasted for two years and three days.

Many people want to see Yolana; she is always in demand and has read for celebrities and statesmen. But she is well worth waiting for.

Glossary of Terms

Most laymen and even some believers are confused about the true meaning of terms frequently used in the field. Others do not fully understand the differences between certain terms, such as ESP and parapsychology, medium and clairvoyant, and so on. For that reason, I have selected the *most commonly used* terms and provided basic explanations for them. Those looking for more sophisticated definitions can find them in books specializing in each subject. For the average reader, however, the following glossary should prove sufficient and helpful.

Some of my explanations may differ from those listed in other sources, especially general encyclopedias or dictionaries. Remember that such general works are not geared to the occult field per se and may contain misinformation or false definitions. Many recent editions of general encyclopedias have, for instance, begun to redefine their explanations of witchcraft, séances, and other basic terms to bring them more in line with current thinking.

Astral Projection. Also called "out of body experience," astral projection refers to the sensation of leaving the physical body, traveling at great speed to distant places, and observing various events, people, and situations. Upon returning to the body, a sensation of falling from great heights is usually present, as the traveling speed of the "inner" or spiritual body is sharply reduced to fit it back into place within the slower, denser physical body. Subjects usually recall their trip in great detail. Astral projection can also be experimentally induced under test conditions. It differs totally from ordinary dreams in that it is a clear, precise memory of having been places. Some astral travelers are as physically tired as if they had really traveled about.

Black Mass. Essentially the product of the bored upper strata of British and French society during the second half of the eighteenth century, this ceremony harks back to the Middle Ages, when it was practiced on rare occasions by anticlerical elements and sometimes by individuals seeking power through it. During the eighteenth century, it was a fashionable thrill. It is rarely practiced today, except by individuals and groups on the fringes of mental aberration.

It consists of a deliberate reversal of the Roman Catholic Mass, from the cross being hung upside down to the litany being said backward. The Black Mass is thought to mock God and Jesus Christ. Witches never practice Black Masses, simply because they do not accept the existence of the Christian religion. They will not mock that which did not exist at the time their cult came into being, thousands of years before Christianity.

Clairvoyance, Clairaudience, Clairsentience. These terms refer to the ability to see, hear, or smell beyond the ordinary five senses. A clairvoyant person foresees events before they happen or while they happen at a distance from the clairvoyant's location. Seeing into the past is also part of this gift, as is the ability to see, hear, or smell events, people, and things not physically present but existing either in another place or on another plane of existence, such as the so-called hereafter.

Control Personality. Trance mediums have guides, sometimes called *controls* or *control personalities*. These are individuals who have died and then attached themselves to the particular medium to help her or him. Their role is much like that of a telephone operator between worlds. Some psychiatrists feel that the controls are in reality split-off parts of the medium's own personality. However, some parapsychologists do accept the individual existence of the controls as independent persons, especially in cases in which the control shows marked personality differences from the medium's own.

Déjà Vu. Literally "already seen," this term means the sudden, fleeting impression many people have of having been to a place, having met someone before, or having heard, seen, or done something before, which in reality they have not. For example, a soldier going overseas for the first time might recognize a certain house in a strange city as if he had been there before. A person might hear himself say something he knows he has said in exactly the same words before but cannot recall when.

The overwhelming number of these déjà vu flashes must be explained as precognitive flashes (*see* Precognition), that is to say, foreknowledge of the event experienced prior to the actual occurrence but unnoticed by the person having the experience at that time. However, when the event becomes objective reality, the fact that one is familiar with the event is realized and the precognitive flash is acknowledged. A smaller percentage of déjà vu experiences, however, clearly indicate partial reincarnation memories.

Dreams. There are four types of dreams: dreams caused by physical stress, such as indigestion; dreams of a psychoanalytical nature expressing suppressed emotions or desires; astral projection dreams (*see* Astral Projection); and psychic or true dreams. In the latter, the sleeper receives specific information about the future, either in the form of a warning of events to come or in the form of a scene showing the event as inevitable. Sometimes deceased individuals make contact with the sleeper in this state because his resistance to receiving communication from the beyond is lower than while fully awake.

Ectoplasm. Examined some years ago at the University of London, ectoplasm turned out to be an albumen substance related to the sexual fluids within the body and secreted by certain glands. It is present during so-called materialization séances (*see* Materialization) and in thinner form also when apparitions occur, as well as in poltergeist (*see* Poltergeist) phenomena, when ectoplasm is formed to move physical objects about. It comes from inside the body of the medium as well as the sitters (*see* Medium and Sitting), and it must be returned to the medium after the experiment to avoid damage to the health of the individuals. Ectoplasm is sensitive to white and yellow light and can exist safely only in dark red illumination.

ESP. The term ESP was coined by Dr. Joseph B. Rhine, formerly of Duke University. Extrasensory perception, in my definition, is the obtaining of information beyond that possible by ordinary means and the five senses as we know them today. It operates through the so-called sixth sense. It is not, in fact, a separate sense but is merely the extension of the five senses beyond what we ordinarily think are their limitations.

Neither extrasensory perception nor the sixth sense implies anything supernatural.

Ether and Etheric Body. Ether in this context is the surrounding atmosphere in the sense that it conducts psychic emanations. Thoughts travel through the ether, and apparitions of the dead exist in the etheric world. The etheric body is the finer, inner body, an exact duplicate of the grosser, outer, or physical body. At death, the etheric body assumes all functions and appearances of the physical shell.

Ghost. Ghosts are the surviving emotional memories of people who have died violently or in some way traumatically and who cannot leave the place of their unexpected or untimely passing. Ghosts are people with their mental faculties severely curtailed, limited to their last impulses, such as some unfinished business or complaint. They are often unaware of their true status, that is, of being outside a physical body. Ghosts neither travel from place to place nor do they normally harm anyone except through fear. The terror ghosts often inspire is unwarranted, since ghosts are entirely occupied with their own problems. These visual images of dead people have been photographed under satisfactory scientific test conditions.

Glossalalia. Also called "speaking with tongues" by religiously oriented researchers, glossalalia is nothing more than the ability of trance. The voice speaking through the entranced person may speak in a language totally unknown to the speaker while in a conscious state, or it may even be a fantasy language.

Hypnosis. In hypnosis, the state of detachment from the conscious self induced by verbal commands or other means, such as sound and light patterns, the subject will do two things: (1) reveal freely his innermost thoughts beyond what he will reveal in the conscious state for various reasons; and (2) accept suggestions he must carry out after he is returned to the normal state. Hypnosis is safe in the hands of medical doctors and of trained psychic researchers when it is also used in reincarnation experiments (*see* Regression). It is not a stage entertainment, although it is often used as such, and even less of a parlor game.

Incantation. In the pagan cults, especially witchcraft, incantations are intense emotional appeals to the deity to do certain things for the petitioner. They are similar to prayers except that they are not dependent on the goodwill of the deity. Incantations always work, in the view of the pagan believer, because they contain just the right formula, just the proper words to "make things happen."

Karma. Not merely an East Indian religious philosophy, but part of the system of reincarnation accepted equally by many people in the Western world, karma is the universal law of rewards for certain actions undertaken in one lifetime but paid off in another. An individual does not generally know what his or her karma from the past consists of; karmic law operates in the way certain opportunities arise in the present life or in the way people meet again who may have known each other in an earlier life. What an individual does of his or her own free will, and from his or her own moral and spiritual resources, will determine the manner in which the karma is "paid off" or extinguished.

Levitation. The ability, often photographed, of physical objects, such as tables and chairs and occasionally even people, to float above the floor for a short time is known as levitation. It is caused by an electromagnetic force field created through the body of a powerful "physical" medium in the immediate vicinity. Great religious ecstasy has on occasion also lowered the weight of a person temporarily so that he would float up to the ceiling. It cannot be reproduced at will, however.

Magic(k). The practical "arm" of witchcraft and other pagan cults, magic is sometimes spelled with a *k* in the antiquated fashion to distinguish it from modern stage magic with which it has nothing in common. It is the better and deeper understanding of the laws of nature beyond that which the average person knows. In this knowledge lie answers to manipulating certain events and people that seem miraculous but are, in effect, perfectly natural.

Materialization. The rare and often imitated ability of producing ectoplasm, which in turn takes on the actual three-dimensional forms of deceased persons, is known as genuine materialization. Experiments have been conducted in England by reputable researchers, usually in rooms illuminated by adequate red light. The materialization medium usually sits in a black "cabinet" or closet, open on one side only. Ectoplasm pours from the mouth and nose of the deeply entranced medium. Genuine materializations rise slowly from the floor and eventually melt back into it when the power fails. Counterfeit materializations, such as have been staged for years in American Spiritualist camps in the summer months, can be spotted fairly easily since the materialized spirit forms walk on and off in their full heights.

Medium. A much misunderstood term, *medium* means intermediary, that is to say, a channel between the world of the living and the world of the dead. It also means a person able to foretell future events and sometimes read the unknown past (*see also* Psychic). Mental mediumship includes clairvoyance, clairaudience, clairsentience, and psychometry, while the much rarer physical mediumship consists of trance and materialization (*see under those headings*). Mediums never "summon" anyone; they merely relate to their clients what communications they receive.

Poltergeist. Formerly thought to be the product of unused sexual energies in pubescent young adults, who cause objects to fly about in destructive ways to attract attention to themselves, the phenomena of poltergeists now are thought by others, including myself, to be part of ghostly manifestations. However, the unused powers of pubescent youngsters, or sometimes of retarded older people, are used by outside forces, generally deceased individuals bent on making their continued presences felt, sometimes in a malevolent fashion.

Precognition. The ability to know ahead of time events transpiring at a later date, or to know something happening a distance away without recourse to the ordinary five senses or any foreknowledge whatever, either consciously or unconsciously, is called precognition.

Premonition. A vague feeling of impending events, usually destructive and sometimes specific in details, a premonition is more often a general misgiving that something bad will happen to someone, including oneself.

Psychic. The term *psychic* (adjective) refers to the broad spectrum of all ESP phenomena, or anything transcending the ordinary five senses. A psychic (noun) is a medium.

Psychometry. Psychometry is the fairly common ability to "read" past, present, or future events involving a person by touching an object owned by that person (preferably something that person alone has owned) and worn on the person, such as a ring, a comb, or a watch. Emotional stimuli coat the object the way a thin coat of silver salts coats a photographic plate. Sensitives can reconstruct events or read them in the future from the touch of the object.

Regression. Hypnotic regression, undertaken by qualified researchers, takes the subject in stages to his or her childhood and then cautiously past birth into an assumed earlier life. The majority of people do not recall any previous incarnation under hypnotic regression even if they consciously would like to.

A few are given to fantasizing to please the hypnotist and will create "lives" in the past. An impressive if small number of individuals have been regressed and found to have had evidential information about previous lives buried deep in their unconscious minds. All of these subjects, however, have had conscious, waking flashes of having been someone else before and were regressed only to deepen the memory of a previous incarnation, not to find it.

Reincarnation. Reincarnation is the conscious existence of a soul in another body and as another person, whether male or female, in a lifetime on earth prior to the present one, and the assumed continuance of that process into another life after the current reincarnation. I have documented several verified cases in *Born Again,* and Dr. Ian Stevenson has done likewise in *Twenty Cases Suggestive of Reincarnation.* Reincarnation applies to everybody, but only a few can recall their previous lives, most notably those whose lives were cut short for one reason or another.

Satanism. The cult of worshipping the devil principle, that is to say, human selfishness, greed, lust, and self-satisfaction, Satanism is a frequently misunderstood and misused word. Modern Satanists, such as Anton LaVey of San Francisco's First Church of Satan, do not deny the existence of the spiritual element in man or the survival of human personality after death. They teach full enjoyment of the physical self, however, and are firmly opposed to charity, compassion, and other unselfish traits. True Satanists, such as exist here and there, are on the fringes of the law and sometimes involve themselves in ritual killings—usually, but not exclusively, of animals. Satanists and devil worshippers have nothing to do with witchcraft, even though they are often confused in the popular mind. Witches and Satanists are in fact opposites.

Séance. The word *séance* means "sitting down" and refers to the assembly of several people for the purpose of spirit communication, psychic development, or other ESP research on a personal basis. Spiritualist séances often involve the holding of hands to create a "circle of power" for a few moments, or the singing of religious hymns to raise the "vibrations" (*see*

Vibrations). Séances can take place in the daytime or at night and are usually held in subdued light. Only in materialization séances do "spirits" appear or objects move. Most séances are intended for verbal communication only, through the mouth of the medium at the head of the table.

Sensitive. When used as a noun, *sensitive* means the same as medium or being a psychic.

Sitting and Sitter. Sitting is a more appropriate term for séance, and a sitter is a person taking part in a sitting or someone consulting a medium privately and individually.

Spell. A spell is a prayer with the force of a directive used in witchcraft and other pagan cults to make certain things happen to another person who is not present when the spell is cast. The specific choice of words, certain ritual actions, and other aids are required to make the spell effective.

Spirit. The "inner self," that which survives physical death of the body, the spirit must not be confused with a ghost, which is an earthbound spirit unable to move on into what Dr. Joseph B. Rhine has called the world of the mind. Spirits are free to come and go; they inhabit the world next to ours in which thoughts are instant action. Spirits are electromagnetic fields formed in the exact duplicate of the person's physical self prior to death, but usually returned to his or her prime state. Thus, spirits, when they appear to the living, usually show themselves in their best years, although they are able to control their appearances at will, being thought forms only.

Spiritualism. Spiritualism is a religion based upon the findings of psychic research and the belief in the continuance of life of the spirit after death of the body. Founded in the 1860s in America and popular also in Great Britain, Spiritualism still flourishes in many subdivisions and sects and is a recognized form of religion. It should not be confused with psychic research or parapsychology, however.

Telekinesis and Teleportation. *Telekinesis* refers to the movement of solid objects by power of mind. This has been done in laboratory experiments at Duke University and recently in Soviet Russia, where it was also recorded photographically. The energy streaming out of the medium's body causes the objects to move. Teleportation is much rarer and less well documented. It involves the sudden and dramatic transportation of solid objects great distances and sometimes through solid objects, utilizing techniques of dematerialization and rematerialization not yet fully understood.

Trance. A trance is a state in which the medium's own personality is temporarily set aside and the spirit or personality of another person is allowed to enter the medium's body and operate the medium's speech mechanism, vocal chords, and facial muscles the way a driver operates an automobile. The driver is not the car, and the medium is not the entity speaking through her. Afterward, the medium does not recall her actions or words while in possession by another being. Trance should only be undertaken in the presence of and under the supervision of a trained psychic researcher.

Transmigration. Transmigration is an East Indian belief that reincarnation is possible between humans and animals. For the present, no evidence for this exists.

Vibrations. Called *vibes* by the young, these are movements of emotionally charged particles filling the ether (*see* Ether) in which we exist. They manifest themselves as emanations, rays, impressions, electromagnetic energy patterns, and so on.

Vision. A visual experience, or vision, concerns events not visible to the eye at the place and time where it occurs. Swedenborg had a vision of the Stockholm fire while a day's journey away. Some visions pertain to future events also.

Witchcraft. Anglo-Saxon/Celtic witchcraft, called *Wicca* or *craft of the wise*, is also known as the Old Religion by its followers. It is a true nature religion based upon three important elements:

1. The firm conviction that reincarnation is a fact and that the cycle of life continues beyond death.
2. The belief in the powers of magic, the better utilization of natural law, to make certain things happen that ordinary people are unable to accomplish.
3. The worship of the Mother Goddess principle of a female deity, representing the creative element in nature, thus free from original sin, guilt, shame, and anything restricting oneself to the narrow limits of an artificially motivated society.

"An' it harm none, do what thou wilt," is the sole law of Wicca.